DEDICATION

For Rob and Sadie with love, as always.

Boston Public Library

100 THINGS TO DO IN MASSACHUSETTS BEFORE YOU DIE

• •

KIM FOLEY MACKINNON

Reedy Press
PO Box 5131
St. Louis, MO 63139, USA
reedypress.com

Library of Congress Control Number: 2024949288

ISBN: 9781681065700

Design by Jill Halpin

Cover photo courtesy of Kim Foley MacKinnon

Unless otherwise noted, all photos are courtesy of the author or believed to be in the public domain.

Printed in the United States of America
25 26 27 28 29 5 4 3 2 1

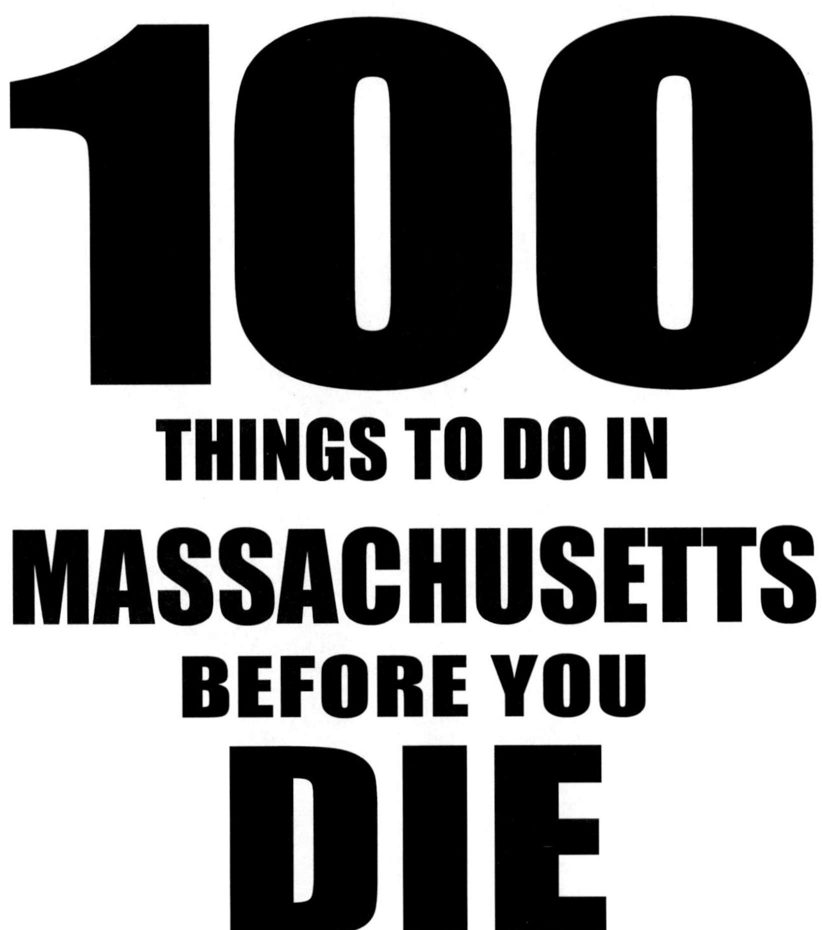

100 THINGS TO DO IN MASSACHUSETTS BEFORE YOU DIE

Shalin Lui
Credit Elizabeth Seitz

CONTENTS

Music and Entertainment

Sports and Recreation

Culture and History

Shopping and Fashion

ACKNOWLEDGMENTS

Books are really a team effort, not the work of one person. My friends and family are always an enormous support system for me, offering ideas, advice, and encouragement. And I never have to ask anyone twice to help me with research on where to eat and drink! A special thanks to Esther Vegh for her excellent proofreading. I am also fortunate enough to have worked with many outstanding public relations people over the years, whose help is invaluable. As always, I have to say thank you to Josh Stevens and everyone at Reedy Press for their support over the years. It's always a pleasure and an honor to work with you all.

Massachusetts State House

PREFACE

It's pretty difficult to reduce an entire state to just 100 things, but it's awfully fun doing the research in the attempt. For this book, I crisscrossed Massachusetts, looking for the iconic places, as well as the unusual, that make the Bay State so unique. The Commonwealth of Massachusetts is the first in so many important events and milestones in our country's history, both large and small, from the "shot heard round the world" to the invention of fried clams. Historic sites, world-class museums, gorgeous green spaces, and events and activities for all seasons—Massachusetts has something for everyone.

Undoubtedly, and maybe obviously, this book is completely subjective. Making the hard choices of what to include means I had to leave some places out. Sometimes when people think of Massachusetts, they focus exclusively on Boston, but there is a whole lot to see and do outside of the capital city (and I did write a book about 100 things to do in Boston!). I hope as you read this book and explore these 100 things, you use it as a launching pad to find even more unique Massachusetts gems.

Sullivan's

FOOD AND DRINK

1

SAMPLE ICONIC PIE
AT PARKER HOUSE

Boston cream pie, the official state dessert of Massachusetts, was invented at the historic Omni Parker House Hotel in Downtown Crossing. Don't expect a traditional version of pie, though, with a flaky crust and maybe a fruit filling. Boston cream pie is more of a custard cake. Its invention, according to the hotel, was in part thanks to easy access to chocolate when America's first chocolate mill opened in Dorchester in 1765. Up to then, New Englanders had typically eaten a dessert called American "pudding-cake pie," but when a Parker House chef drizzled chocolate icing onto it, history was made.

The hotel, which opened in 1885, is the longest continuously operating hotel in the United States and has lots of other claims to fame. Fluffy and delicious Parker House rolls were also invented there, and all sorts of famous people have worked at the hotel, such as Emeril Lagasse, Malcolm X, and Ho Chi Minh.

60 School St., Boston, 617-227-8600
omnihotels.com/hotels/boston-parker-house/dining/parkers-restaurant

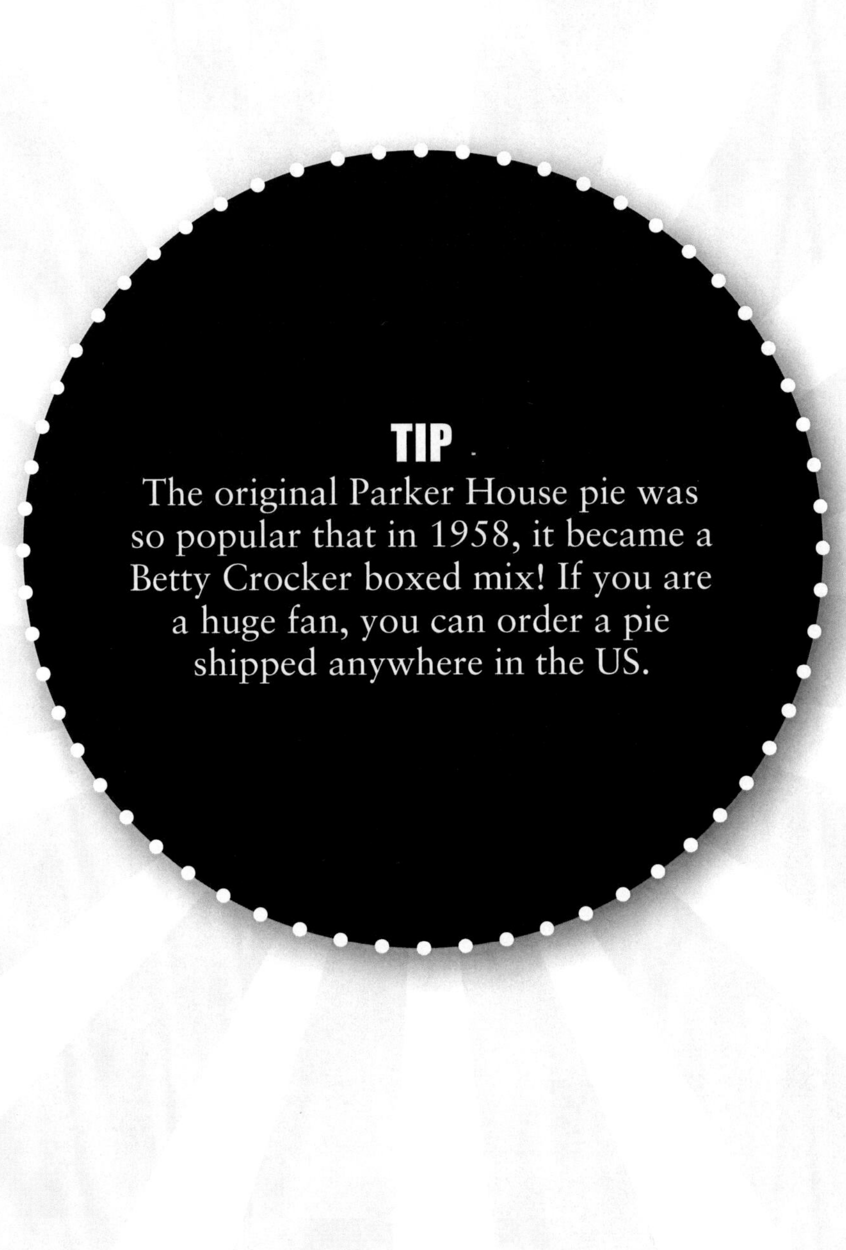

TIP

The original Parker House pie was so popular that in 1958, it became a Betty Crocker boxed mix! If you are a huge fan, you can order a pie shipped anywhere in the US.

2

GO LOCAL
AT BOSTON PUBLIC MARKET

Want to support New England makers, eat delicious food, buy artisanal products, and sip on local beverages all at the same time? It's easier to do than you might think. The nonprofit Boston Public Market, located next to Haymarket Station across from the Rose Kennedy Greenway, has you covered. Everything at the lively venue is made in Massachusetts or New England, with about 30 vendors under one roof. Tempting food stations offer everything from pastrami sandwiches to piping hot popovers, along with lobster rolls, doughnuts, fresh produce, and more. Sidle up to the Pine Bar and grab a drink before perusing the market. You can also pick up beverages to go at Boston Beer Alley, with its excellent curated selection of craft beers, handcrafted liquor, spirits, and cider. A slate of ongoing events includes tastings, trivia, sing-alongs, demos, crafting, and other fun activities.

100 Hanover St., Boston, 617-973-4909
bostonpublicmarket.org

TIP

There is an outpost of the market at Boston Logan International Airport in Terminal C.

DON'T MISS THESE FIVE SPOTS IN THE MARKET

Curio Spice Co.

Ethically sourced spices, salt blends, and teas from small-scale spice farmers.

Laurel Greenfield Art

This local artist offers fun paintings and prints of food memories from New England and beyond.

Peterman's Boards and Bowls

Gorgeous bowls, serving boards, napkin rings, and more made from discarded or fallen trees from New England towns.

tiny farmhouse

Environmentally responsible stationery, home goods, and accessories with original illustrations and patterns.

Parlott Chocolatier

Handcrafted truffles, chocolate bars, barks, and assorted candies.

3

MAKE A BEELINE
FOR BELKIN FAMILY LOOKOUT FARM

One of the oldest continuously working farms in the United States is found in Natick, about 30 minutes from Boston. You can easily enjoy a whole day of fun at the property. Start picking whatever happens to be in season at the 180-acre farm, which grows about two dozen apple varietals plus peaches, pears, nectarines, strawberries, plums, pumpkins, and hops. Head to the beer garden or the taproom to enjoy beer or cider brewed on-site and order from a pretty extensive food menu. In good weather, park yourself at one of the many picnic tables in the garden and enjoy everything from fried pickles to burgers to barbecue ribs. The farm also offers brunch on the weekend, and there's a market if you'd rather not pick your own fruit. Fresh apple cider donuts are also available for as long as they last, which is never very long!

89 Pleasant St., South Natick, 508-745-3697
lookoutfarm.com

OTHER MASSACHUSETTS PICK-YOUR-OWN FARMS

Ward's Berry Farm

614 S Main St., Sharon, 781-784-3600
wardsberryfarm.com

Parlee Farms

95 Farwell Rd., Tyngsboro, 978-649-3854
parleefarms.com

Verrill Farm

11 Wheeler Rd., Concord, 978-369-4494
verrillfarm.com

Coonamessett

277 Hatchville Rd., East Falmouth, 508-563-2560
coonamessettfarm.com

Tougas Family Farm

234 Ball St., Northborough, 508-393-6406
tougasfamilyfarm.com

4

SAVOR SEAFOOD AND HISTORY
AT THE UNION OYSTER HOUSE

Established in 1826, the Union Oyster House is a National Historic Landmark and the oldest continuously run restaurant in the United States. Sit at the famous U-shaped oyster bar, where Daniel Webster used to sit drinking brandy and water, downing oysters by the half dozen (allegedly he would have six plates a day!), and see if you can match his appetite. Get the longtime shuckers, some of whom have been there for years, if not decades, talking and you may hear some amusing stories. Other famous faces at the restaurant over the years include a veritable who's who, such as Franklin Roosevelt, John F. Kennedy, and Bill Clinton, plus plenty of governors, athletes, and movie stars. Other favorite items on the menu include the house clam chowder, fish and chips, broiled Boston scrod, and lobster. Make sure to poke around the warren of dining rooms, with wooden stalls and seating that seem unchanged from the day the restaurant opened.

41 Union St., Boston, 617-227-2750
unionoysterhouse.com

MORE HISTORIC BOSTON RESTAURANTS AND PUBS

Warren Tavern

2 Pleasant St., Charlestown, 617-241-8142
warrentavern.com

Bell in Hand

45 Union St., Boston, 617-227-2098
thebellinhand.com

The Green Dragon Tavern

11 Marshall St., Boston, 617-367-0055
greendragonboston.com

OAK Long Bar + Kitchen

138 St. James Ave., Boston, 617-585-7222
www.oaklongbarkitchen.com

LEG IT
TO LEGAL SEA FOODS

Almost as ubiquitous as the Dunkin' franchise in New England, Legal Sea Foods restaurants can be found all over Massachusetts and as far away as Illinois. The founders, the Berkowitz family, opened a fish market in Cambridge in 1950 and then, in 1968, opened their first restaurant. The Legal name became synonymous with fresh fish, and its popularity just grew and grew. The tagline "If it isn't fresh, it isn't Legal!" became well known, and its renowned clam chowder has been served at almost every presidential inauguration since 1981.

There are many Legal spots to choose from (including at Logan airport), but the chain's flagship restaurant, Legal Harborside, in the Seaport District overlooking the harbor, is the most scenic. The third-floor, four-season roof deck called Overlook has a retractable glass roof and walls so you can enjoy gorgeous views along with your chowder, lobster, or other seafood favorites.

270 Northern Ave., Boston, 617-477-2900
legalseafoods.com

6

CATCH THE FRESH
AT JAMES HOOK & CO.

If you ask a group of Bostonians where to get the best lobster roll in the city, you won't hear the same answer twice, but for a classic version with a side of history, you can't beat old-school James Hook & Co. on Boston Harbor. The lobster-centric menu features lobster rolls, buttered or with mayo; whole cooked lobsters; lobster mac and cheese; and lobster salad, as well as clam chowder, stuffed clams, and crab cakes.

For 100 years, the Hook family has been supplying freshly caught lobster to Boston and beyond. Founded in 1925 by James Hook and his three sons, Edward, James, and Alfred, the business grew by leaps and bounds, selling wholesale lobster near and far. Now it's run by four siblings of the third generation of the Hook family, and in addition to the brisk business at its waterfront shop and restaurant, the family ships more than 50,000 pounds of lobster daily.

440 Atlantic Ave., Boston, 617-423-5501
jameshooklobster.com

EAT LIKE YOU'RE IN ITALY IN THE NORTH END

The North End, often referred to as Boston's "Little Italy," is a tiny neighborhood next to Boston Harbor packed with Italian restaurants, cafés, pizzerias, specialty grocers, bakeries, gelaterias, shops, and more. It's Boston's oldest residential neighborhood and perhaps its most densely packed. Don't drive here—take the T. It's more fun to explore on foot, anyway.

Go down all the side streets, even the alleys. One hidden gem is a bread shop down a side alley, down a flight of stairs. See if you can find this bakery that supplies several neighborhood restaurants. There's a famous fan rivalry between Mike's Pastry and Modern Pastry Shop, across the street from each other, but you can't go wrong with cannoli from either. Popular restaurants include Bricco, Villa Francesca, and Neptune Oyster, but these just scratch the surface. Part of the fun of visiting the North End is finding your own favorite spot. Many restaurants don't serve dessert and instead encourage you to explore and find a small café for coffee, cake, or gelato.

North End, Boston
boston.gov/neighborhood/north-end

NORTH END HIGHLIGHTS

Bova's Bakery

134 Salem St., 617-523-5601
bovabakeryboston.net

Galleria Umberto

289 Hanover St., 617-227-5709

Mamma Maria

3 North Square, 617-523-0077
mammamaria.com

Regina Pizzeria

11 1/2 Thacher St., 617-227-0765
reginapizzeria.com/north_end.html

Caffé Vittoria

290–296 Hanover St., 617-227-7606
www.caffevittoria.com

8

DIG INTO A DOG
AT SULLY'S

Since 1951, Sullivan's, located at Castle Island in South Boston, right next to Fort Independence, has offered tasty food to generations of families. The quick-service spot offers everything from hot dogs to lobster rolls to ice cream. Its crinkle cut french fries are a specialty, and the hand-cut onion rings are addictive. You can join the line to order, then take your food to a park bench or find a picnic spot near the fort to watch the planes coming and going from Logan airport. This is a perfect location for plane-spotting.

Castle Island and Fort Independence (built between 1834 and 1851) is a 22-acre urban park, with walkways connecting to Pleasure Bay, the M Street Beach, and Carson Beach, so it's easy to make a whole day of it if you want. In warmer months, the Castle Island Association gives free tours of the historic fort.

2080 William J. Day Blvd., Boston, 617-268-5685
sullivanscastleisland.com

JOIN THE CROWD
AT J. J. FOLEY'S CAFÉ

Since 1909, this family-owned-and-operated Irish pub in the South End has been serving beers and bites in an authentic and warmly welcoming setting. Foley's is Boston's oldest pub, and all sorts of historic meetings and gatherings have taken place under its roof over the years, from politicians campaigning to newspaper staff and police officers unwinding after their shifts and sharing stories.

To this day, white-button shirts and ties are sported by the bartenders, who are consummate professionals. There is always a Foley on hand to keep an eye on things (there are several in the family, no relation to author). Classic pub food, along with pastas, pizzas, steaks, and seafood, is on the dining menu, while Guinness, of course, with a variety of drafts, bottles, and a full bar, is available for drinks. The South End has changed quite a bit over the years, but even gentrification can't take away Foley's down-to-earth vibe.

117 E Berkeley St., Boston, 617-728-9101
jjfoleyscafe.com

10

TASTE TEST
AT TIME OUT MARKET BOSTON

This fun Fenway food hall, one of eight markets from the famous media brand found around the world (with more locations scheduled), is a great place to sample dishes from some of Boston's finest chefs in a casual setting. Eating at the market can be faster and less expensive than dining in their restaurants, too. Big names like chef Michael Schlow have outlets here. Try his famous rigatoni with spicy sausage ragu, or maybe you'd prefer Japanese-style chicken and dumplings from Ms. Clucks Deluxe, owned by James Beard Award–winning chef Tim Cushman. He and his wife, Nancy, an advanced sake professional, also own the acclaimed restaurants o ya and Hojoko. There's a full bar inside, with local brewery Trillium outside. Other options include Union Square Donuts, Far Out Ice Cream, and Squeeze Juice Co., among others, which should satisfy all appetites. In addition, events at the market include book signings, flea markets, DJs, tastings, and more.

401 Park Dr., Boston, 978-393-8088
timeoutmarket.com/boston

ROAM THE HALLS

In recent years, Boston has had an explosion of food halls. Here are a few more to check out in the city.

Hub Hall

Located next to TD Garden and North Station, with world-class ramen from chef Masaharu Morimoto at Momosan and iconic Boston favorites like Sullivan's Castle Island lobster rolls and cannoli from Mike's Pastry.

80 Causeway St., Boston, 617-263-8900
hubhallboston.com

High Street Place

Near South Station, this place offers more than a dozen venues, including a few from famed chef Tiffani Faison, including Tenderoni's Pizza. Other venues include an Asian fusion "lab" and Sugar Skulls, serving ice cream tacos, boozy floats, and frozen cocktails.

100 High St., Boston
highstreetplace.com

Eataly

A playground for Italian foodies, this three-story venue in the Back Bay boasts everything from a butcher to a bakery, four full-service restaurants, and casual food counters. Shelves are stocked with specialty wines, chocolates, housewares, oils, fresh seafood, and more.

800 Boylston St., Boston, 617-807-7300
eataly.com

11

DINE ON AUTHENTIC FARE
IN CHINATOWN

Said to be the third largest in the United States, Boston's Chinatown is small but densely packed with shops and restaurants, located between Downtown Crossing and South Station. The neighborhood was settled by Chinese immigrants in the 1870s, and waves of immigration from several regions in China and across Asia have made their way here over the years. Look for the colorful three-story pagoda-style arch at the end of Beach Street, which signals you are in the right place.

Whatever type of Asian cuisine you desire, from dim sum extravaganzas on weekends to mooncakes at traditional bakeries to bubble tea cafés, you can find it here. Popular spots for dining include Empire Garden, Hei La Moon, Peach Farm, and Jumbo Seafood. May's Cake House and 180 Café are famous for their baked goods. You will also find shops specializing in herbs, gifts, clothing, and more. Wandering around the neighborhood, popping into places that appeal to you, is the best way to visit.

chinatownmainstreet.org

TIP
To take a deeper dive into Chinatown, take a guided tour. The Original Chinatown Tour (bostonchinatowntours.com) and Bites of Boston (bitesofbostonfoodtours.com) are excellent options for eating and learning.

12

TIPPLE
AT TRURO VINEYARDS

This Cape Cod winery and distillery, a family-owned-and-operated business that opened in 1991, produces more than a dozen varietals and grows chardonnay, cabernet franc, and merlot grapes, all of which are handpicked at harvest time. In addition, the family operates a distillery on the property called South Hollow Spirits, the first legal distillery in operation on Cape Cod since Prohibition. The land Truro sits on has been in use since at least 1813 and even inspired the artist Edward Hopper to paint both the 19th-century Federal house and its barn in 1930.

It's lots of fun to visit the winery, which offers wine and spirits tastings, plus you can picnic on the grounds and relax in Adirondack chairs. You can order wine and drinks, peruse the well-stocked shop, and order from local food trucks, which are often on-site. Events range from paint-and-sip classes to live music and festivals.

11 Shore Rd. (Rte. 6A), North Truro, 508-487-6200
trurovineyardsofcapecod.com

DOWN A DRAFT
AT DORCHESTER BREWING

Dorchester Brewing Co. (DBC) is a lively space, with several floors to check out, from the "Hopservatory," its four-season rooftop greenhouse, with an outdoor patio overlooking the Boston skyline, to the well-stocked Game Room, with pinball, Skee-Ball, shuffleboard, and more. DBC serves both in-house and partner brews, with 20 taps, plus hard cider, hard slushies, seltzers, wine, cider, and nonalcoholic drinks. The in-house restaurant, M&M BBQ, serves up tasty ribs, mac and cheese, corn bread, and other delicious Southern fare, along with fries, pretzels, wings, and other bar food.

If you love quirky attractions, the brewery is also home to the Museum of Bad Art, which displays "art too bad to be ignored." This offbeat nonprofit organization, formed in 1993, has moved locations over the years but seems to have found a permanent home here. Browsing the "art" with a beer can be a hilarious endeavor.

1250 Massachusetts Ave., Dorchester, 617-514-0900
dorchesterbrewing.com

FEAST ON FRIED CLAMS
AT WOODMAN'S

Like so many of the best food origin stories, the one about how fried clams were invented seems almost too corny to be true, but this one has plenty of proof. Lawrence "Chubby" Woodman and his wife, Bessie, opened a small concession stand on Main Street in Essex, selling fresh clams dug by Chubby, homemade potato chips, and other grocery items. On July 3, 1916, as the story goes, Chubby was complaining about slow business, and a friend jokingly said he should fry up some clams. Bessie and Chubby took it seriously, though, experimented with batters, and debuted fried clams the next day at the town's Fourth of July parade. Within a year, copycats were serving them everywhere, and even Howard Johnson (yes, that one!) came calling to learn how to make them. Five generations later, the family is still serving them to the crowds that pack the restaurant for the tasty, crispy clams, as well as other seafood dishes.

119 Main St., Essex, 978-768-6451
woodmans.com

CLAMS, CLAMS, AND MORE CLAMS

Woodman's may have invented the fried clam, but several spots on the North Shore hold their own in the market. As with lobster rolls, many people will vigorously defend their favorite place. Why not do a sampling and find yours?

Clam Box

246 High St., Ipswich, 978-356-9707
clamboxipswich.com

J. T. Farnham's

88 Eastern Ave., Essex, 978-768-6643
jtfarnhams-essex.com

Essex Seafood

143 Eastern Ave., Essex, 978-768-7233
facebook.com/EsxSfdRestaurant

TRY A NEW BREW
AT TRILLIUM

The wildly popular Trillium Brewing Company, opened in 2016 by J. C. and Esther Tetreault, may have started small, but boy has it grown. Today, it has multiple locations to enjoy its craft beers in and around Boston. Its massive brewery, restaurant, and taproom in Canton offers indoor and plenty of outdoor seating, with beer and food trucks outside. Inside you can sit at the long bar and watch the cooks make delicious wood-fired pizzas as you sip a brew or snack on other items. Music and trivia nights are part of the entertainment offered.

You can also find branches of Trillium in Fort Point and Fenway, plus seasonal beer gardens at the Rose Kennedy Greenway and Boston Common. Trillium is very forward-thinking, with innovative programs such as carbon dioxide recapture. It is also hyperlocal, with its own farm, and the company works with dozens of New England vendors to source local ingredients.

100 Royall St., Canton, 781-562-0073
trilliumbrewing.com

16

INDULGE IN OYSTERS
AT ISLAND CREEK

Oyster lovers in Massachusetts are well-acquainted with Island Creek Oysters, which can be found on menus all over the state (and elsewhere), but the company's large complex in Duxbury is like a playground for seafood foodies. There are three different opportunities for indulging. One is the Raw Bar, a casual indoor/outdoor waterfront venue, with two floors, multiple bars, and a menu with oysters, of course, plus other snacks, local craft beer, wines, and nonalcoholic drinks.

Across the street, you'll find the delightful Winsor House, Island Creek's food and hospitality flagship. The charming spot is warm and welcoming, with farmhouse vibes and a full menu. There's an adorable bar and seating out back, too. Finally, you can book a tour to see where all the oyster magic starts. You will visit the hatchery, take a boat ride around Duxbury Bay, and eat as many oysters as you can handle.

403 Washington St., Duxbury, 781-934-2028
shop.islandcreekoysters.com

TIP

If you take an oyster farm tour, you can BYOB!

17

SCREAM FOR ICE CREAM
AT KIMBALL FARM

Kimball Farm, a family-owned operation that started in 1939, is synonymous with ice cream and fun. Today, it has four locations around the state and in New Hampshire, but the main Westford campus is where you'll find the center of all the activities, especially in the height of summer. Besides more than 50 flavors of delicious homemade ice cream to sample, there's an outdoor grill and seafood shack, a country store, and 50 acres packed with everything from mini golf to bumper boats to batting cages. There's also a zip line, an arcade, pony rides, and an animal rescue center, to name a few more attractions. And that's not all! There's a summer music series, too. While ice cream is Kimball's claim to fame, frozen yogurt, sorbet, sherbet, and even vegan ice cream are also available, so no one is left out.

400 Littleton Rd. (Rte. 110), Westford, 978-486-3891
kimballfarm.com

18

STEP BACK IN TIME
AT PUBLICK HOUSE HISTORIC INN

The Publick House Historic Inn in Sturbridge has a long history dating back to the 1770s. Revolutionary War troops were among its visitors, as were the Marquis de Lafayette and his son, Georges Washington de Lafayette, who toured the nation during the 1820s. The inn's fortunes have waxed and waned over the years, but today it is quite a beautiful complex, with several different types of accommodations.

The Historic Tap Room is the inn's original dining room, with an impressive six-foot open-hearth fireplace. Ebenezer's Tavern is named for the founder and first keeper of the inn, Colonel Ebenezer Crafts. Each venue makes you feel as if you have stepped back in time, with 18th-century decor and wooden floors and chairs. Menus also embrace a traditional New England vibe, with a roasted turkey dinner, Yankee pot roast, baked scrod, and the like. You can also get a treat to take away at the old-fashioned Bake Shoppe next to the tavern.

277 Main St. (Rte. 131), Sturbridge, 508-347-3313
publickhouse.com

DRINK A DRAFT
AT TREE HOUSE

Craft breweries are not rare anymore, but not many achieve cult status. Tree House Brewing Company, which began in a small barn in Brimfield, is now a national award-winning brewery. It has several venues, but its main hub and flagship is in Charlton, which is massive, with plenty of indoor and outdoor seating and a shop. There's a pavilion outside with a couple of fireplaces, and clusters of Adirondack chairs are scattered around the property, where you can relax with your beverage. And yes, dogs (and kids) are welcome.

Julius, its signature IPA, is what put the brewery on the map, but it has dozens of varieties to choose from, as well as spirits, cold brews, and seltzers. Other locations include a brewery in Deerfield; a taproom and brewery on Cape Cod; a golf course and taproom in Tewksbury; and a fermentory in Woodstock, Connecticut.

129 Sturbridge Rd., Charlton, 413-523-2367
treehousebrew.com

20

EMBRACE BBQ
AT BUB'S

No one could assert that Massachusetts is any sort of barbecue center, but Bub's, opened in 1979 by Howard "Bub" Tiley, is one of the more authentic barbecue joints in the region. Certainly, Bub's vision of southern barbecue has had staying power. Today this humble-looking spot in the Pioneer Valley in western Mass is still plating up smoky racks of ribs, pulled pork, beef brisket, chicken, and more, plus fried catfish, shrimp, and sides of mac and cheese, collards, sweet potato casserole, and other favorite Southern dishes. As befits a barbecue joint, this is a casual spot, with picnic tables outside, as well as on a covered porch, with more seating inside. You order at the counter, wait for your food to be plated, then find your seat. The restaurant also has a breakfast buffet on weekends.

676 Amherst Rd., Sunderland, 413-548-9630
bubsbbq.com

21

LINE UP

FOR LOBSTER AT LARSEN'S

Larsen's Fish Market offers one of the best and freshest lobster rolls in the state, and in a picture-perfect spot that looks like it's from Hollywood central casting. Located on Martha's Vineyard in the small fishing village of Menemsha, Larsen's was opened in 1969 by Louis Larsen, an offshore fisherman, and his wife, Mary. Eventually their daughters Betsy and Kristine began working there, and by age 19, Betsy was running the whole shebang. Today, much of the family still works there. You can pick up the freshest seafood to cook at home or order from a small menu and eat it on the spot outside on a bench. My go-to here is the lobster roll, made with freshly caught lobster, loaded onto a hot dog roll and doused with hot butter. It's sublime. You can also get whole steamed lobsters, freshly shucked oysters, crab cakes, and more from the small kitchen.

56 Basin Rd., Chilmark, 508-645-2680
larsensfishmarket.com

TIP

Menemsha Public Beach is a prime spot to watch the sunset. BYOB, chairs or a blanket, plus seafood from the market, and enjoy an unforgettable meal and a show.

Grace by Nia

MUSIC
AND ENTERTAINMENT

HEAR MUSIC
AT SYMPHONY HALL

Not only is Boston Symphony Hall a place to hear world-class music, it's also an architectural and acoustical gem. Opened in 1900, the hall was the first auditorium to be designed in accordance with scientifically derived acoustical principles. A mathematical formula was developed so that an ideal reverberation time of 1.9 to 2.1 seconds could be achieved. To focus the sound on the main seating areas, an optimal shape was selected for the concert hall. The walls of the stage slope inward to help focus the sound of the orchestra.

Take a free behind-the-scenes tour to learn about the construction, as well as elements inside, such as the 16 replicas of Greek and Roman statues, which draw upon music, art, and literature references. The Symphony Hall organ, an Aeolian-Skinner designed by G. Donald Harrison, was installed in 1949 and is considered one of the finest in the world. Of course, attending a concert is the best way to appreciate the hall!

301 Massachusetts Ave., Boston, 617-266-1492
bso.org

23

OPEN YOUR EARS

AT THE OPERA HOUSE

Opened in 1928 as the B. F. Keith Memorial Theatre, the Citizens Opera House was originally named for Benjamin Franklin Keith, the famous vaudeville impresario of the late 1800s and early 1900s. It's a gorgeous example of a vaudeville circuit palace, a fitting home for such a popular form of entertainment in its time. It was designed with a combination of French and Italian styles by Thomas White Lamb, the foremost theater architect of the era.

Restored to its glory in 2004, it offers a regal theater setting with clear sight lines and near-perfect acoustics for a variety of performances. Today, productions range from shows like *Les Misérables* to *Mamma Mia!* to *Funny Girl*. The Boston Ballet performs its iconic *The Nutcracker* at the gorgeous venue every year, as well as other ballets throughout the year.

539 Washington St., Boston, 617-259-3400
citizensoperahouse.com

TIP

If you want to learn more about the theater, you can take a tour, offered several times a week.

24

BOP OVER
TO THE BOCH CENTER

The nonprofit Boch Center oversees two historic properties in the Theater District, the Wang and Shubert Theatres, which have history dating back 100-plus years. The Wang, listed on the National Register of Historic Places, opened as the Metropolitan Theatre in 1925. The Shubert opened in 1910 as a stage for Shakespeare plays, then evolved as a venue for pre-Broadway tryouts. Today, both venues offer a variety of shows from plays to concerts to comedy acts.

If you can't catch a show, take a behind-the-scenes tour at the Wang Theatre, where you'll get an overview of the historic architectural highlights and unique history, from its hotel roots and glamorous days when it served as a movie "cathedral." The venue is also home to the Folk Americana Roots Hall of Fame (folkamericanarootshalloffame.org), which features exhibits and memorabilia about these musical genres and performers.

265 & 270 Tremont St., Boston
bochcenter.org

JAM
AT WALLY'S CAFÉ JAZZ CLUB

Since 1947, this small jazz club in the South End, the first Black-owned club in New England, has been a draw for musicians and music lovers alike. The historic family-owned spot is considered a training ground for many aspiring music students attending local institutions such as Berklee College of Music and the Boston Conservatory, and plenty of professional musicians perform here, too.

The club is open every day of the year, and there are three sets each night, from 5 to 7 p.m., 7 to 9 p.m., and 9 p.m. to 1 a.m. The first set is usually a jam session, with the second and third sets having different themes. Monday is blues; Tuesday, Wednesday, and Sunday are funk; Thursday is Latin jazz salsa; and Friday and Saturday are jazz. There is never a cover charge, and you never know which talented new performer might just be the next big thing or what famous musician might pop in to play.

427 Massachusetts Ave., Boston, 617-424-1408
wallyscafe.com

26

BUZZ OVER
TO THE BEEHIVE

Channeling Bohemian vibes, the Beehive, located in the South End, is a fun and lively spot to eat, drink, and hear free live music every night of the week. Situated in the Boston Center for the Arts complex, the large, artsy, two-story restaurant and club is decorated with colorful works from local artists. There are lots of different spaces to kick back and take in the live entertainment, from table-side to barstools.

The music is wide ranging, from jazz to blues, cabaret to burlesque, country to R & B. On weekends, there's also live music during brunch, from 10 a.m. to 2 p.m. Sunday night is blues night, with Bruce Bears & Friends from 7:30 to 10:30 p.m. Band leader Bruce Bears has been a renowned figured in the international blues scene for decades, and he brings in an impressive roster of local and international talent.

541 Tremont St., Boston, 617-423-0069
beehiveboston.com

27

CLAP YOUR HANDS
AT SCULLERS JAZZ CLUB

Scullers Jazz Club, located on the ground floor of the DoubleTree Suites, has been a music mainstay since 1989. What's fun about Scullers is that it feels like an old-time jazz club, where patrons dress up a little and everyone is seated at tables, all of which have great sight lines of the musicians. Over the years, big names like Harry Connick Jr., Tony Bennett, Lisa Fischer, Michael Bublé, and Wynton Marsalis, as well as up-and-coming acts, have played here. Diana Krall, Norah Jones, and Peter Cincotti were introduced on the Scullers stage.

In general, there are two shows on Friday and Saturday nights, at 7 and 9 p.m. There's a full bar and food menu if you want to make it a dinner-and-show occasion. Before the first show, you can also book a ticket for the preshow reception, which includes small plates, a carving station, dessert, and parking. The hotel offers special overnight packages, too.

400 Soldiers Field Rd., Boston, 617-562-4111
scullersjazz.com

TAP YOUR TOES
AT REGATTABAR

Located in Cambridge on the third floor of the Charles Hotel, Regattabar opened to the public in 1985. Like many performance venues, it closed its doors during the pandemic, and it seemed like it might never return. So a collective sigh of relief went up from the jazz community when the intimate 220-seat venue reopened in the fall of 2023.

Big names such as Dizzy Gillespie and Herbie Hancock have graced the stage, but many aspiring performers have launched from the club. There's a full bar and a menu of light bites, such as cheese and charcuterie boards, that you can enjoy during the show. Or dine at one of the hotel's three restaurants (at Henrietta's Table, you will receive 10 percent off the tab with your ticket).

1 Bennett St., Cambridge, 617-661-5000
regattabarjazz.com

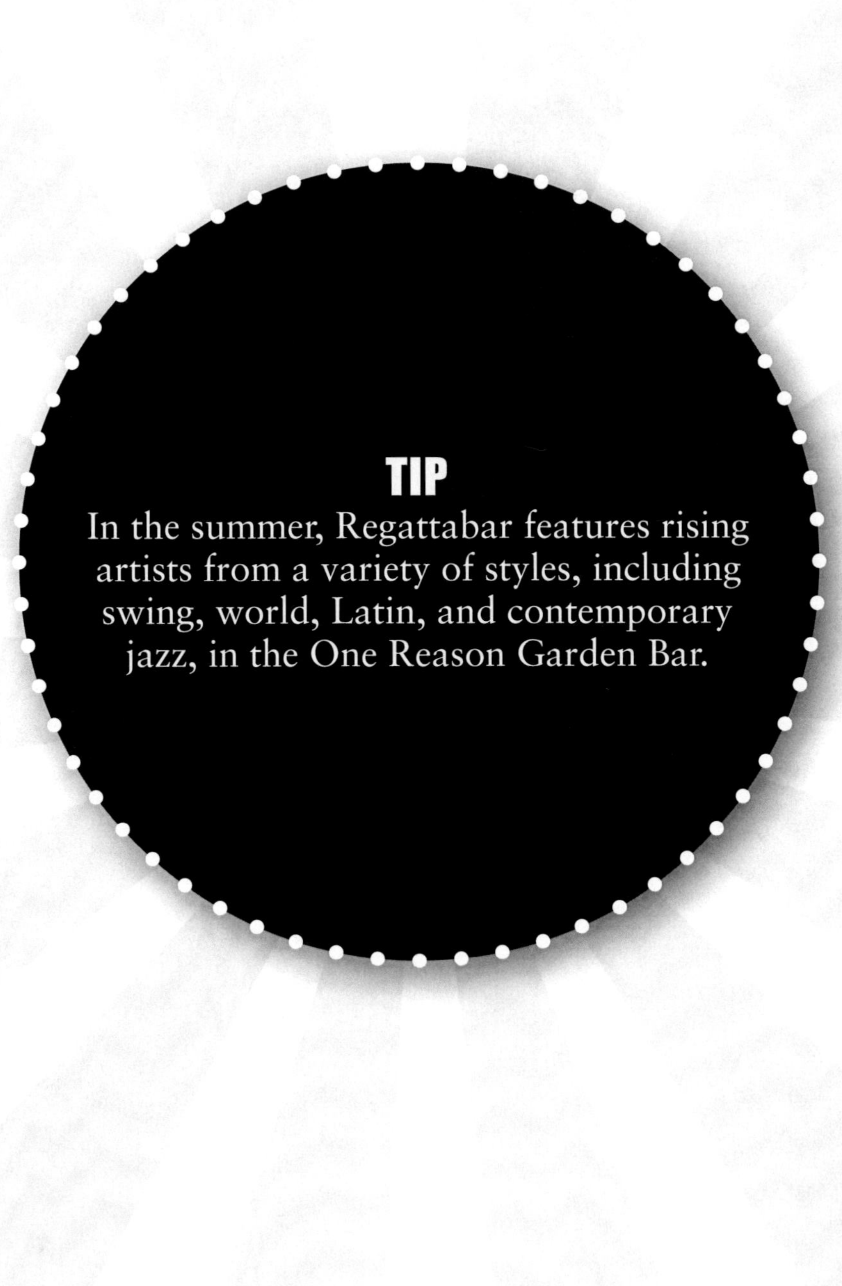
TIP
In the summer, Regattabar features rising artists from a variety of styles, including swing, world, Latin, and contemporary jazz, in the One Reason Garden Bar.

GROOVE OUT
AT GRACE BY NIA

Nia Grace is a successful local restaurateur, and this supper club in the Seaport is her latest establishment, in partnership with the Big Night Entertainment Group, which owns several other venues (Empire, Scorpion Bar, and the Grand). Giant brass palm trees and dramatic lighting greet you upon entering the space. The vibe is upscale, and people dress to impress. There is live music every night, with a focus on soul, R & B, and reggae. You can opt to sit at the bar or in the dining room, but the small round stage-side tables near the band are the best seats in the house. The food menu offers Southern fare, with dishes like fried catfish, bourbon peach ribs, and mac and cheese. Reservations are highly recommended, and depending on where you are seated, a different entertainment fee will be added to your bill. It's definitely a great place for dinner and a show.

60 Seaport Blvd., Boston, 617-927-9411
gracebynia.com

SCAN THE SKYLINE
AT VIEW BOSTON

Head to the top of the Prudential Tower for unparalleled 360-degree views of Boston and beyond at View Boston, which features indoor and outdoor viewing areas, an open-air observation deck, two dining outlets, and state-of-the-art immersive experiential exhibits spread out over three floors. After getting your fill of the views from the 52nd floor, check out digital maps that allow you to zoom in on places you want to learn about, and check out other informative displays about the city.

The 51st floor, called the Cloud Terrace, is an open-air deck, with an indoor/outdoor cocktail bar called Stratus. For a heartier meal, the Beacon restaurant serves typical New England fare, with the same breathtaking views. An immersive 270-degree theater offers a street-level view of various neighborhoods and behind-the-scenes perspectives of some of Boston's most popular attractions, including Fenway Park. Few city observatories have outdoor platforms, so View Boston's is uncommonly memorable.

800 Boylston St., Boston, 617-544-3535
viewboston.com

ROCK OUT
AT INDIAN RANCH

Located on the shores of Lake Chargoggagoggmanchaugga-goggchaubunagungamaugg (good luck saying that!), Indian Ranch has been a popular outdoor music venue since 1946. In its early years, it was known as the "Nashville of the North," with acts such as Johnny Cash, Willie Nelson, Loretta Lynn, and Charlie Daniels hitting the stage. Over time, more music genres have been added, including classic rock, pop, roots rock, and blues. Among the acts who have appeared are Barenaked Ladies, Huey Lewis and the News, B. B. King, the Mavericks, Pat Benatar, the Beach Boys, and others.

You can make a full day of visiting preconcert if you like, swimming in the lake or chilling on the beach, and dining at the ranch's signature restaurant, Samuel Slater. You can also go for a ride on the *Indian Princess*, an authentic paddlewheel riverboat. And rest assured, you don't have to use the full lake name; most people just call it Lake Webster.

200 Gore Rd., Webster, 508-943-3871
indianranch.com

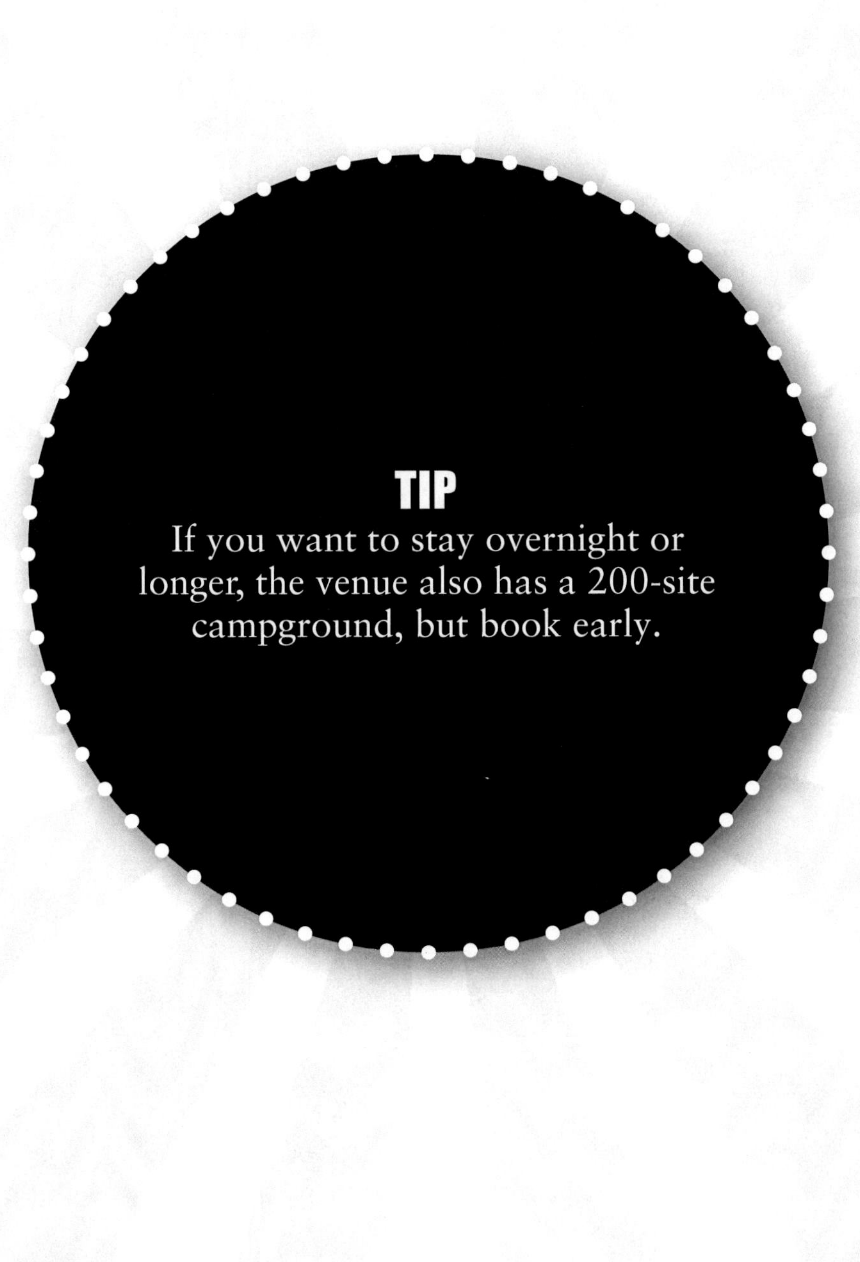
TIP
If you want to stay overnight or longer, the venue also has a 200-site campground, but book early.

32

SURVEY SIX STATES
AT THE BIG E

Formally named the Eastern States Exposition, the "Big E" is the largest expo on the East Coast and the seventh-largest fair in North America. It's held for two weeks in the fall, and instead of focusing on a single state, it features six New England states, making it one of a kind. Head to the Avenues of the States, where you can see and walk through replica statehouses of Massachusetts, Maine, Vermont, New Hampshire, Connecticut, and Rhode Island. What's more, each building sits on land actually owned by that state. Inside, you'll find food, drinks, products, and displays from each state.

But this area is just the tip of the iceberg at the fair. Everything from a big top to parades to big-name performers to food, shops, rides, and a reconstructed village of nine authentic 18th- and 19th-century buildings makes the event an extravaganza of sights and sounds. When you go, you'll want to wear your most comfortable walking shoes.

1305 Memorial Ave., West Springfield, 413-737-2443
thebige.com

DRESS UP
FOR KING RICHARD'S FAIRE

Who doesn't want to pretend to be royalty for a day, a turkey leg in one hand and a mead in the other? King Richard's Faire, which is held in Carver weekends from late August through October, is one of New England's largest renaissance festivals. Visitors are encouraged to come in costume, and plenty do, to enjoy medieval entertainment, arts, and food on the 80-acre site. Jousting tournaments by the king's knights on horseback, plus hundreds of performers dressed as minstrels, acrobats, fire eaters, aerialists, and larger-than-life-size puppets, entertain the masses.

You can try your hand at archery, axe throwing, and other games; get your face or body painted; shop for period leather, armor, and footwear; and take in contests and shows on the fair's eight stages. You can also get a tarot card reading, browse jewelry stands, get a temporary tattoo, and just eat, drink, and be merry.

235 Main St., Carver, 952-238-9915
kingrichardsfaire.net

34

TAKE A TRIP
TO TANGLEWOOD

Tanglewood, located on a 500-acre property between Lenox and Stockbridge, is the summer home of the Boston Symphony Orchestra and the Boston Pops. In a typical season, more than 350,000 people come for world-class performances, recitals, and seminars. Concerts are held in the 5,000-seat main shed and lawn, while the more intimate 1,200-seat Seiji Ozawa Hall is used for chamber music and solo performances.

Highlights of every season include the annual Tanglewood on Parade; in 2024, it was dedicated to famed conductor Seiji Ozawa. Popular artists have included Judy Collins, the Indigo Girls, and Rufus Wainwright. Having a picnic on the lawn while listening to a concert is an idyllic summer activity. If you don't want to pack your own, you can order one in advance from a venue at Tanglewood, complete with a table and cushions, plus beverage service. There are several other dining options, too.

297 West St., Lenox, 617-266-1492
bso.org/tanglewood

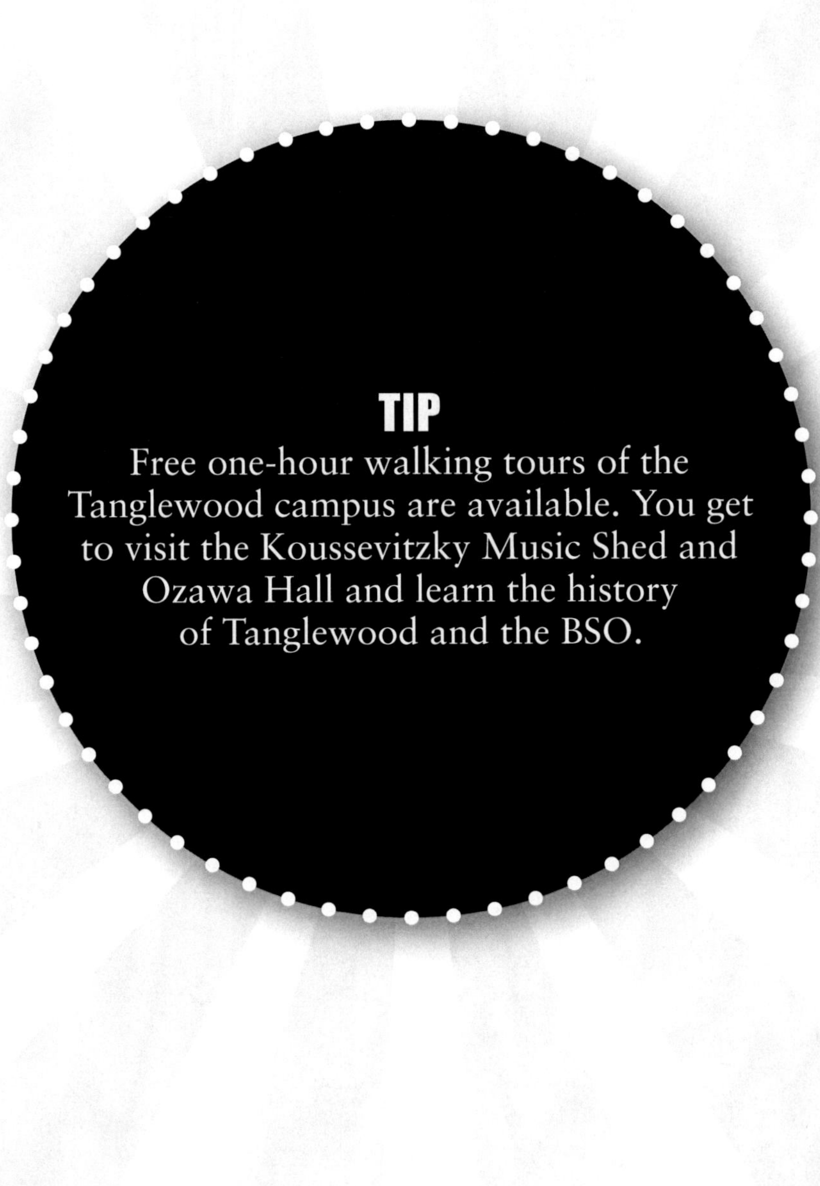
TIP
Free one-hour walking tours of the Tanglewood campus are available. You get to visit the Koussevitzky Music Shed and Ozawa Hall and learn the history of Tanglewood and the BSO.

SLIP UP
TO SHALIN LUI

Rockport Music has one of the most beautiful venues to hear music anywhere: its intimate Shalin Liu Performance Center, with 330 seats, sits on Rockport Harbor, and the view is simply stunning. The backdrop of the ocean, seen through a wall of glass behind the performers, adds a dramatic touch that is almost magical to see.

The center, which opened in 2010, was designed to showcase chamber music and, more specifically, the organization's signature Rockport Chamber Music Festival, which includes more than 20 concerts, as well as lectures, open rehearsals, and events. Rockport Music actually dates back more than four decades, when it focused solely on chamber music. It has broadened its scope over the years to include classical, jazz, folk, and pop music; HD broadcasts from the Metropolitan Opera and England's National Theatre; and films. When you attend a concert or other event here, it always feels quite special.

37 Main St., Rockport, 978-546-7391
rockportmusic.org

JUMP
TO JACOB'S PILLOW

The Jacob's Pillow Dance Festival is another beloved summertime tradition in the Berkshires, with a showcase of world-renowned ballet, modern, and international dance performers. It's the country's longest-running international dance festival and a recipient of the National Medal of Arts. The 220-acre National Historic Landmark grounds are lovely to explore, too.

Over the course of the summer, more than 50 dance companies come to participate, and there are more than 500 free performances, talks, and events open to the public. Performances take place at the Ted Shawn Theatre and the outdoor Henry J. Leir Stage. Workshops, tours, exhibits, pop-up performances, dance parties, and the chance to see rehearsals at the prestigious School at Jacob's Pillow are all part of the festival lineup. There's also a café, pub, and coffee shop on the grounds, and like Tanglewood, you can order a picnic to enjoy on the lawn.

358 George Carter Rd., Becket, 413-243-0745
jacobspillow.org

SEE A SHOW
ON THE SOUTH SHORE

The Music Circus and Melody Tent, owned and operated by the nonprofit South Shore Playhouse Associates, have a history dating back more than 60 years on Cape Cod. They are also the only two continuously operated tent theaters-in-the-round in the United States. Both venues have attracted major stars of the stage and film, as well as patrons, who love that every seat is within 50 feet of the stage.

Among the famous names who have performed at one venue or the other are Ginger Rogers, Bob Hope, Debbie Reynolds, Tony Bennett, Linda Ronstadt, B. B. King, Alice Cooper, Willie Nelson, Hall & Oates, the Indigo Girls, Ani DiFranco, Aimee Mann, and Aretha Franklin. Plays, musicals, tribute bands, and comedians also perform on the stages. Tickets are reasonably priced, especially considering the caliber of the star power you can see.

Music Circus
130 Sohier St., Cohasset, 781-383-9850
themusiccircus.org

Melody Tent
41 W Main St., Hyannis, 508-775-5630
melodytent.org

WATCH A MOVIE
AT THE WELLFLEET DRIVE-IN

The Wellfleet Drive-In Theatre, in business since 1957, is a Cape Cod mainstay and one of about 300 drive-ins still operating in the country. Generations of families have made this a favorite part of their summers (it's generally open May through September). While the drive-in is a classic, its technology is all modern. First-run double features play on a 100-by-44-foot screen, with an FM stereo sound system equipped with Dolby Digital sound. For those who prefer air conditioning or go during the off-season, there's an indoor cinema with four screens that is open year-round.

Besides movies, the drive-in hosts the Cape's largest flea market, where about 200 vendors offer everything from Cape Cod memorabilia to T-shirts, antiques, jewelry, and other knickknacks. There is also a playground, a vintage 18-hole miniature golf course built in 1961, a dairy bar, and a snack bar. A beer and wine garden is open outside the snack bar during the flea market only.

51 State Hwy. (Rte. 6), Wellfleet, 508-349-7176
wellfleetcinemas.com

FROLIC
AT THE FAIR

The sweet and long-running annual Martha's Vineyard Agricultural Society Livestock Show and Fair, or the "Ag Fair," was started in 1859 as a one-day event but has grown to four full days of celebrating everything agricultural, with a side of carnival fun. From racing pigs and tractor pulls to rides, games, fried dough, and corn dogs, it's everything you could want in a bucolic county fair. The event is traditionally held the third week of August and is a highlight of the summer for many residents and visitors.

The old-fashioned fair feels like a wonderful throwback. See sheep-shearing demos, watch the parade of oxen in the pulling ring, go to the chopstick knitting contest, or listen to live music. There's a women's skillet toss, a kids' corn husking competition, and sack races, to name a few of the good-hearted games. Head to the barn to see the prize rabbits, chickens, goats, and other animals from youth groups, as well as adults hoping for a blue ribbon.

35 Panhandle Rd., West Tisbury, 508-693-9549
marthasvineyardagriculturalsociety.org

40

BOOGIE ALL NIGHT
AT THE BEACHCOMBER

This famous Cape Cod restaurant/bar/nightclub, located in a former US Life-Saving Service station at Cahoon Hollow Beach in Wellfleet, has been a draw for more than a generation of beach lovers and partygoers. The building dates back to 1897 and was one of nine Life-Saving Service stations built on the Outer Cape. In 1953, Russell Gallagher, who had summered in the area as a child, bought it and turned it into a small inn named the Beachcomber. Over the years, it evolved into the much larger, iconic spot it is now, with a lively scene most summer nights.

Freshly shucked oysters, boozy frozen mudslides, and awesome live music bring people in by the droves. During the day, it's kid-friendly, with families enjoying the beach and eating at the excellent restaurant, which offers the freshest seafood. But at night, it's adults-only for live music, DJs, dancing, and good times.

1120 Cahoon Hollow Rd., Wellfleet, 508-349-6055
thebeachcomber.com

MassMutual
FENWAY PARK
newbalance
CLEAResult
WELCOME TO FENWAY PARK
AMERICA'S MOST BELOVED BALLPARK
APRIL 16, 2024
Ford
TRULY
ĀURA
IRVING
420
jetBlue
GRANITE CITY
79
Fenway Park

SPORTS AND RECREATION

SEEK SERENITY
IN THE EMERALD NECKLACE

Boston's Emerald Necklace is a series of parks, running seven miles end to end, covering 1,100 acres, and connecting the city's green spaces. Renowned landscape architect Frederick Law Olmsted, who also designed New York's Central Park (among others), laid the groundwork for the system in the late 19th century to give city folks places to enjoy nature. Franklin Park, Arnold Arboretum, Jamaica Pond, Olmsted Park, the Riverway, Back Bay Fens, Commonwealth Avenue Mall, the Public Garden, and Boston Common make up the Emerald Necklace.

Opportunities for recreation include walking along shady paths, rowing or sailing on Jamaica Pond, and playing golf or visiting the zoo at Franklin Park. Historic homes, gorgeous gardens, and scenic footpaths make exploring fun. The Emerald Necklace Conservancy provides walking and cycling tours, plus maps, exhibits, and other info from its visitor center in the Back Bay Fens.

Shattuck Visitor Center
125 the Fenway, Boston, 617-522-2700
emeraldnecklace.org

42

FERRY OVER
TO THE BOSTON HARBOR ISLANDS

A short ride away from the city is one of Boston's lesser-known attractions, the Boston Harbor Islands National and State Park, which is composed of 34 islands and peninsulas. The two islands most people gravitate to are Georges and Spectacle, as they have the most amenities. Georges is home to Fort Warren, a spooky Civil War–era fort you can explore. Spectacle Island has served as farmland, a quarantine hospital, a glue factory, a resort, and a landfill, and now offers a beach with lifeguards, 2.5 miles of trails, and the highest viewing point of any of the islands, at 155 feet. It is a great place for photos of Boston.

Activities on various islands include the nation's oldest continuously used light station, clambakes, live musical performances, vintage 1860s baseball games, and overnight camping. Ferries run from May through October. If time is short, even a round trip on the ferry is worth it for the views.

Boston Harbor Islands, 617-223-8666
bostonharborislands.org

WADE
INTO WALDEN POND

One of the pivotal figures of Early American literature, Henry David Thoreau, made his home next to Walden Pond in Concord, going to live and work there in 1845. He stayed for two years in a one-room cabin, keeping a journal of his thoughts and his encounters with nature and society. Eventually, he published them in his book *Walden* in 1854. Today, the pond is part of the 462-acre Walden Pond State Reservation, where visitors can enjoy both nature and history. Besides swimming in the pond, which is actually a 103-foot-deep kettle hole, you can picnic, hike, canoe, row, fish, cross-country ski, and snowshoe. The site of Thoreau's original house is staked out in stone, and you can visit the full-size, authentically furnished replica of the cabin, located near the parking lot. Rangers offer interpretive programs, with guided walks, poetry readings, and crafts.

915 Walden St. (Rte. 126), Concord, 978-369-3254
mass.gov/locations/walden-pond-state-reservation

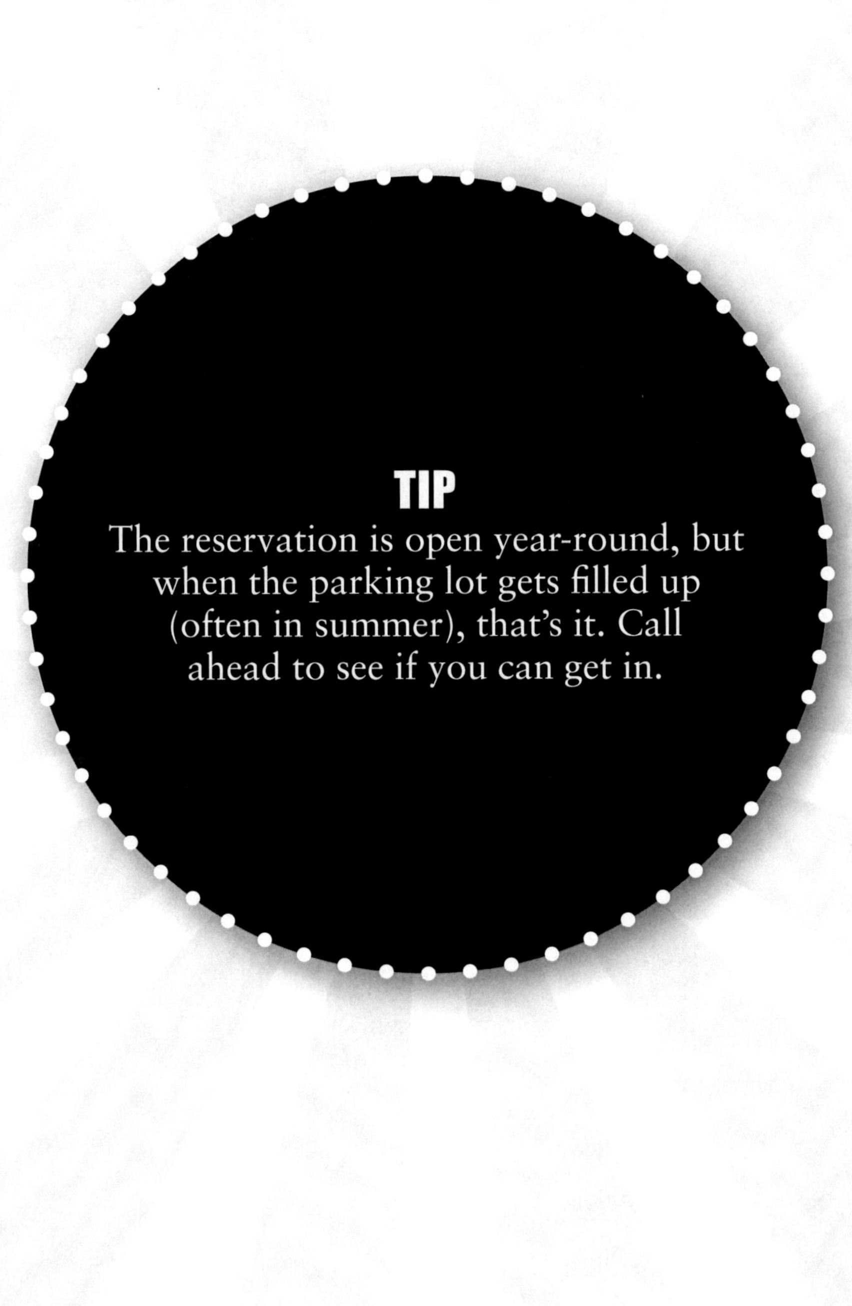
TIP
The reservation is open year-round, but when the parking lot gets filled up (often in summer), that's it. Call ahead to see if you can get in.

GALLIVANT AROUND
THE ROSE KENNEDY GREENWAY

This 1.5-mile-long park, which goes through several Boston waterfront neighborhoods, offers a lot to enjoy, including artwork, live performances, farmers markets, beer gardens, outdoor movies, temporary exhibits, and fitness classes, to name a few activities. A mix of different food trucks rotate around the Greenway, so visitors can always find something tasty to eat. There are also seven fountains, a labyrinth, and a New England–themed carousel, which instead of horses features a codfish, a seal, a peregrine falcon, a sea turtle, a lobster, a green grasshopper, and a whimsical sea creature. What makes the park even better is that it replaced an elevated highway, long an eyesore that broke up neighborhoods.

And the "green" in Greenway is taken very seriously. The park is one of the only public parks in the region maintained completely organically, with no synthetic fertilizers, chemicals, or pesticides. There are also beehives, a wildflower meadow, and a pollinator garden.

From the North End to Chinatown, Boston, 617-292-0020
rosekennedygreenway.org

HEAD FOR
THE (BLUE) HILLS

The 7,000-acre-plus Blue Hills Reservation, which was set aside for public recreation in 1893, crosses several towns, including Quincy, Dedham, Milton, and Randolph. Great Blue Hill reaches a height of 635 feet, the highest of the 22 hills in the Blue Hills chain, and the Blue Hills Weather Observatory, a National Historic Landmark, sits atop the summit (and is open for tours).

The reservation is a playground for outdoors lovers, with 125 miles of trails, where you can hike, bike, rock climb, ski, swim, kayak, and much more. Sixteen historic structures detail the stories of Native Americans, explorers, farmers, quarry workers, and inventors from the region. A good place to start your visit is the Mass Audubon Blue Hills Trailside Museum, which serves as the welcome center for the reservation and has a natural history museum, with indoor and outdoor live animal exhibits. You can pick up maps and get the lay of the land here.

725 Hillside St., Milton, 617-698-1802
mass.gov/locations/blue-hills-reservation

BE A FAN
AT FENWAY PARK

America's oldest Major League Baseball park, where the Red Sox have played since 1912, is hallowed ground for baseball fans. For an in-depth look at the stadium, you can take one of several guided tours, which are offered year-round. Highlights include seeing where Ted Williams's famous 502-foot home run landed, learning about Pesky's Pole, and getting onto the field.

One of the stadium's most iconic features is the world-famous Green Monster, which stands 37 feet, 2 inches high overlooking left field. It's just over 300 feet from home plate and in the field of play, so deep fly balls that would have been outs in other parks sometimes become home runs. Rex Sox Nation, as fans are called, sing "Take Me Out to the Ball Game" during the seventh-inning stretch, as well as Neil Diamond's "Sweet Caroline" at the bottom of the eighth. If the Sox win, the Standells' "Dirty Water" blasts over the loudspeakers.

4 Jersey St., Boston, 617-226-6666
mlb.com

TIP

If you can't get tickets ahead of time, try your luck 90 minutes before the game at the stadium, when a few tickets are sold. Or you can head to the Bleacher Bar (82A Lansdowne St.), where a huge window overlooks center field.

47

CELEBRATE SPORTS
AT THE GARDEN

You don't have to be a Boston sports fan to appreciate all the history that has happened in the "Garden," or more formally, the TD Garden North arena. To visit the Sports Museum, you have to take a one-hour guided tour (the only option) to enjoy a variety of exhibits and the opportunity to explore part of the Garden. Highlights include a tribute to the "Impossible Dream" 1967 Red Sox, and Boston's most recent sports champions, the 2024 Celtics.

At the end of the tour, the guide drops you off in the Boston Bruins Heritage Hall, an immersive experience into the 100-year history of one of the NHL's flagship franchises, where you can explore on your own. There's a film about the history of the Bruins, more than 65 iconic Bruins artifacts and pieces of memorabilia, a replica interactive NESN broadcast desk, hockey simulators where you can try your shooting skills, and more.

TD Garden, 100 Legends Way, Boston, 617-212-6814
sportsmuseum.org

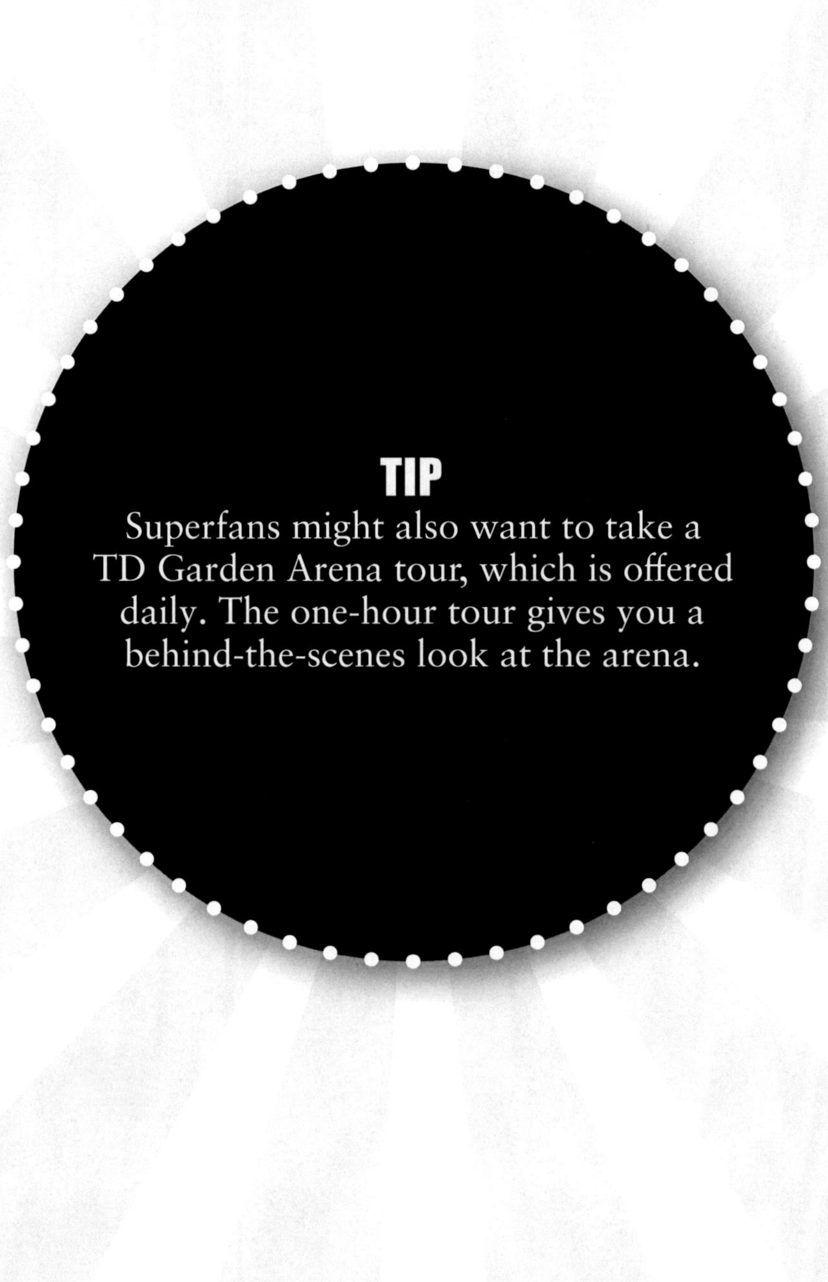

TIP

Superfans might also want to take a TD Garden Arena tour, which is offered daily. The one-hour tour gives you a behind-the-scenes look at the arena.

SPEND A DAY
AT THE SEASHORE

Established in 1961 by President John F. Kennedy, the Cape Cod National Seashore, which runs from Chatham to Provincetown, with 40 miles of coastline and about 45,000 acres of land, is one of Massachusetts's most special places. There are beaches, dunes, marshes, ponds, forests, cranberry bogs, and historical sites to explore, with activities like swimming, hiking, fishing, boating, and so much more. Visiting lighthouses, taking ranger-led talks or guided tours, and whale-watching will educate you about the region and its history. You can also head out on self-guided nature trails, and there are great bicycle paths.

Start your day at the Salt Pond Visitor Center in Eastham, where you can get your bearings and pick up maps, talk to rangers, watch an orientation movie, and visit the bookstore and museum. Note that from late June through Labor Day, and weekends from Memorial Day through mid-September, there are entrance fees at the park beaches, Coast Guard, Nauset Light, Marconi, Head of the Meadow, Race Point, and Herring Cove.

50 Nauset Rd., Eastham, 508-255-3421
nps.gov/caco

PAY HOMAGE
AT PATRIOTS HALL OF FAME

A shrine to all things Patriots, this museum goes way over the top, beginning with the Patriots helmet tunnel, which re-creates the experience the football team used to have—for years, the Patriots ran through an inflated Patriots helmet as they entered their home field. This tunnel leads to the Patriots United Grand Hall, and you'll hear audio as you walk through, with crowd noises getting louder and louder, as if you were about to run onto the field.

Exhibits in the 20,000-square-foot space include the RTX Theater, Building Blocks, the Changing Exhibit, New England Football, In the Numbers, By the Numbers, and special displays. Don't miss the *Patriots Way* film, an 18-minute panoramic feature that connects the New England region to its football team. In the Building Blocks exhibit, look for the three interactive touch-screen kiosks that present comprehensive information on every Patriots team in history, including hundreds of rare photos and video clips.

1 Patriot Place, Foxborough, 508-698-4800
patriotshalloffame.com

MAKE TIME
FOR MINUTE MAN

This 1,000-acre park encompasses many important people, places, and moments in the opening battles of the American Revolution on April 19, 1775, and beyond. Start your visit at the Minute Man Visitor Center in Lexington, where you can pick up guides and see the free presentation, "The Road to Revolution," a comprehensive look at the events of April 1775. In Concord, you can visit North Bridge, the site of "the shot heard round the world."

Walk along the Battle Road Trail, a five-mile trail that connects historic sites from Meriam's Corner in Concord to the boundary of the park in Lexington. You can also make stops at historic Hartwell Tavern and the Wayside in Concord, which during the Revolutionary era was the home of Samuel Whitney, muster master of the Concord Minute Men. In the 19th century, three famous authors, Louisa May Alcott, Nathaniel Hawthorne, and Harriett Lothrop (Margaret Sidney), lived there at different times.

North Bridge/Park Headquarters
174 Liberty St., Concord, 978 369-6993
nps.gov/mima/index.htm

BOUNCE OVER
TO THE BASKETBALL HALL OF FAME

In 1891, challenged to create a new game for restless students at Springfield College to play indoors during the winter, a 31-year-old physical education graduate student named James Naismith incorporated techniques from a variety of other games of the time to draft something new. In one fateful and humorous moment, when Naismith asked a janitor for two boxes to use as goals, he received two peach baskets instead. “Basket ball” was born!

Fast-forward to present day and the impressive Naismith Memorial Basketball Hall of Fame, which you can’t miss, since part of the building is an enormous silver basketball-shaped sphere. It celebrates all aspects of the game. There are excellent interactive exhibits; the Hall of Honor for award winners; and thousands of artifacts, memorabilia, films, and photos. You can even try your hand throwing balls on the full-size Jerry Colangelo “Court of Dreams.”

1000 Hall of Fame Ave., Springfield, 877-446-6752
hoophall.com

CAPER AROUND
THE CRANE ESTATE

The story of the Crane Estate in Ipswich begins with J. B. Brown, who in the 1880s turned Castle Hill Farm from an agricultural holding into a gentleman's farm. In 1910, Chicago industrialist Richard Teller Crane Jr., heir to Crane Co., and his wife, Florence Higinbotham Crane, purchased the property and transformed it into one of America's great summer country estates. Today, the Crane Estate is owned and run by the nonprofit Trustees of Reservations and comprises 2,100 acres of the Crane family's original 3,500-acre estate, with Castle Hill, Crane Beach, and the Crane Wildlife Refuge. All can be enjoyed by the public.

Take a tour of Castle Hill, a Stuart-style mansion that was designated a National Historic Landmark in 1998. Or head to the gorgeous Crane Beach for a day of sun, or to the Crane Wildlife Refuge, with coastal and island habitats, which can be explored on foot or by boat.

290 Argilla Rd., Ipswich, 978-356-4351
thetrustees.org/place/castle-hill-on-the-crane-estate

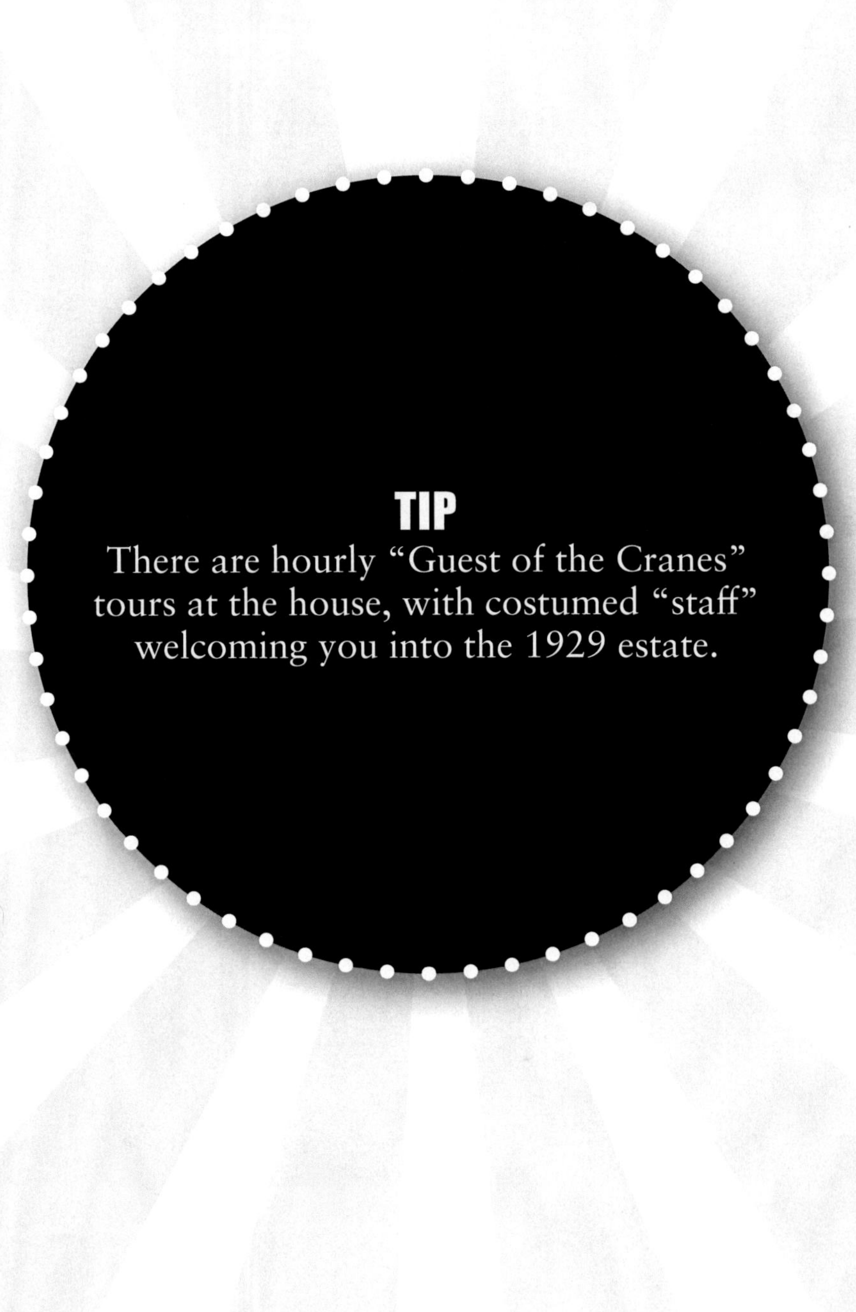

TIP

There are hourly "Guest of the Cranes" tours at the house, with costumed "staff" welcoming you into the 1929 estate.

MOSEY ON
THE MOHAWK TRAIL

The Mohawk Trail, a designated National Scenic Byway in Western Massachusetts, stretches 63 miles on an east–west route. The trail dates back to long before European settlers arrived and was originally a footpath for the peoples of the northeast between the Connecticut and Hudson River Valleys. The trail became the first scenic road in New England in 1914. Today, it leads you through several towns, with dozens of attractions to visit, including historic sites, museums, theaters, and all sorts of outdoor activities. Many people love to just drive along the route in the fall and leaf-peep.

While there are too many places to see to list here, two bridges on the trail are of note. One is the Bridge of Flowers in Shelburne Falls, a former trolley bridge that crosses the Deerfield River that was turned into a gorgeous garden pedestrian bridge. The other is North America's only natural white marble arch, found in Natural Bridge State Park in North Adams.

Mohawk Trail Region, 413-743-8127
mohawktrail.com

Make a stop at Hairpin Turn, a nail-biting section of the road in Clarksburg, for absolutely stunning panoramic views in all directions. You can also enjoy a meal or a drink with the view at the historic Golden Eagle restaurant, which sits on the curve and opened in 1914.

54

MARVEL FOR MILES
FROM MOUNT GREYLOCK

Acquired by the Commonwealth of Massachusetts in 1898, the 10,000-acre-plus Mount Greylock State Reservation was the state's first national wilderness park, and Mount Greylock, at 3,491 feet, is the highest point in Massachusetts. On a clear day, you may be able to see up to 90 miles away. You can do every sort of outdoor activity here, including cycling, fishing, horseback riding, camping, and snowmobiling. Without a doubt, though, hiking is a major draw, and a portion of the Appalachian Trail passes through it.

Stop in at the reservation's visitor center, where you can look at interpretive exhibits, which describe the area through artifacts and displays. You can also pick up trail maps, get hike guidance from rangers, and watch a 13-minute orientation film. In the summer, a variety of programs and guided tours are offered, including summit tours, geocaching, photo walks, and nighttime owl prowls.

30 Rockwell Rd., Lanesborough, 413-499-4262
mass.gov/locations/mount-greylock-state-reservation

STOP AND SMELL THE FLOWERS
AT THE BOTANIC GARDEN

The 200-acre New England Botanic Garden at Tower Hill in Boylston is owned and operated by one of the oldest horticultural societies in the country, the Worcester County Horticultural Society, which began in 1842. The lovely property features a variety of gardens, plus a café and a shop. You can easily spend a day roaming around, and each visit is different, depending upon the season.

Sections include the Ramble, a whimsical space for families with interactive play features; the Court: A Garden Within Reach, which is a multisensory accessible garden with raised beds, living walls, and plants; the Inner Park, a five-acre woodland native plant garden; the Vegetable Garden, with heirloom vegetables, fruits, and herbs; the Lawn Garden, with thousands of spring bulbs and summer-blooming perennials; and the Orangerie and Limonaia, which are conservatories home to collections of non-hardy plants, such as citrus, palms, camellias, and orchids.

11 French Dr., Boylston, 508-869-6111
nebg.org

DIVE INTO
NORTH SHORE BEACHES

Cape Cod gets a lot of love for its beaches, but there is no denying that the North Shore has its own gorgeous beaches, too. In high summer season, it takes a little advance planning to get parking passes online, and you may have to arrive early to get a space, but it's well worth it. Good Harbor Beach in Gloucester, surrounded by grassy dunes, has soft sand and calm waters. Long Beach is another soft-sand beach, half in Rockport, half in Gloucester. Wingaersheek Beach in Gloucester may be the most popular of the North Shore beaches, with white sand for miles and dunes in a well-protected cove. When it's low tide, you can head out to a sandbar for awesome views. Singing Beach, in Manchester, is named for the squeaky noise the sand makes underfoot and is quite special. There are several other beaches in the region, which are equally beautiful, if not as well known.

Gloucester, Rockport, and Manchester
northofboston.org/beaches-lighthouses

From Memorial Day through mid-September, parking reservations must be made online in advance for most of the beaches. Visit the North of Boston website, which has links to the various parking portals.

WANDER
WORLD'S END

This 250-acre property, owned and managed by the nonprofit Trustees of Reservations, is just about 15 miles from Boston and offers amazing views of the city skyline. Now a sanctuary, it narrowly missed being a residential subdivision in the late 1800s, the United Nations headquarters in the 1940s, and a nuclear power plant in the 1960s. In 1967, the Trustees bought the land, and now everyone can enjoy the saltwater marshes, meadows, and woodlands.

Some interesting features make up the property. When wealthy Boston businessman John Brewer bought the estate in the 1880s, he hired landscape architect Frederick Law Olmsted to plan a 163-home residential subdivision. While the homes were never built, a little over four miles of carriage roads Olmsted designed remain to this day and are great for walking, snowshoeing, and cross-country skiing.

Martins Lane, Hingham, 781-740-6665
thetrustees.org/place/worlds-end-hingham

Mount Greylock

Woodman's

OMAN'S
SSEX
1914

Rose K. Greenway

JFK Museum

Island Creek

OYSTERS

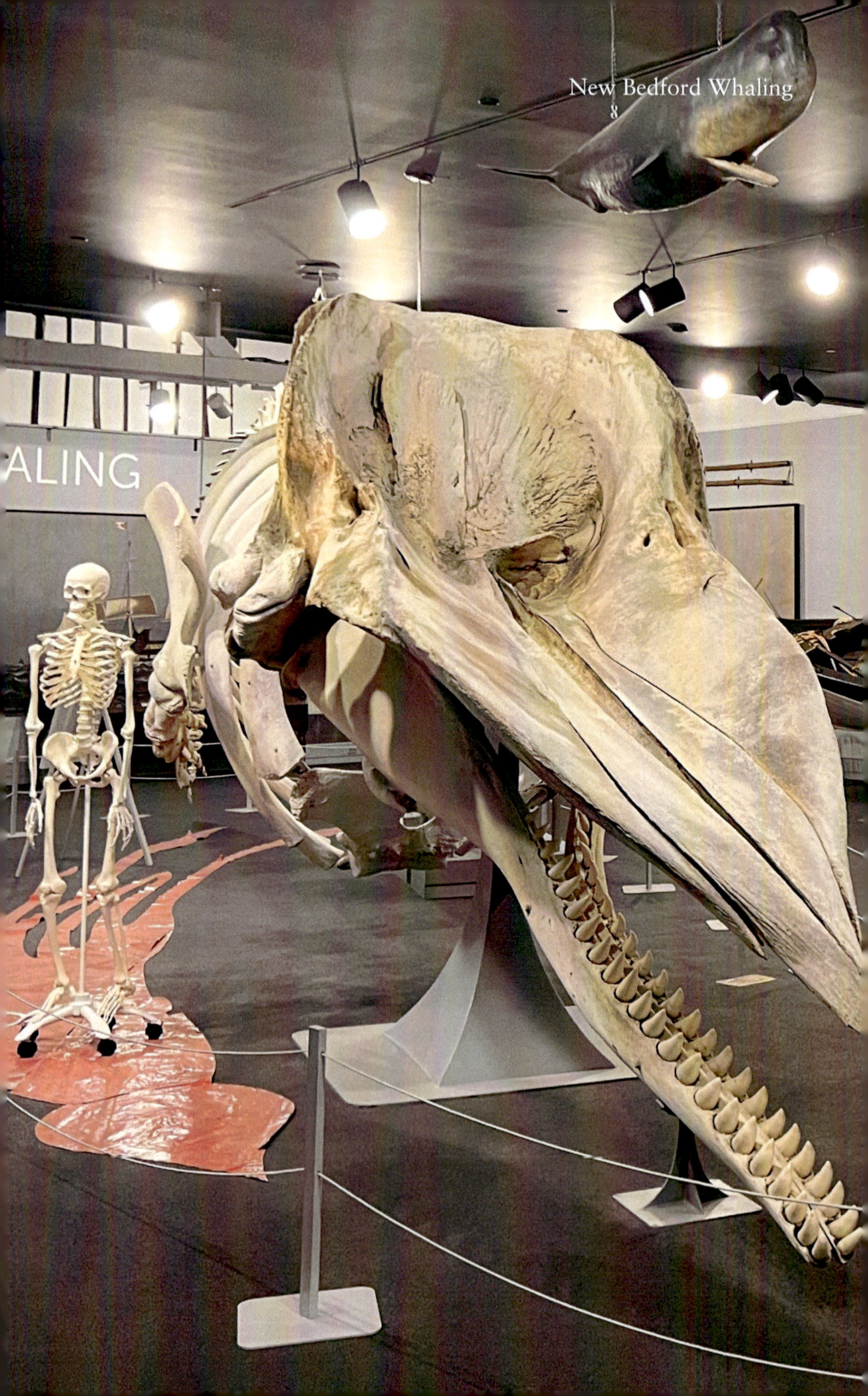
ALING

Beacon Hill Books

Rocky Neck

Edgartown Lighthouse

Tea Party Ships

Salem

Boston Seaport

High Street Place Food Hall

VAULT OVER
TO THE VOLLEYBALL HALL OF FAME

Western Mass is not just where basketball was invented; volleyball was invented in this part of the state, too. Generally accepted as being created in 1895 in Holyoke, the game, like basketball, was designed to fill a need for a noncontact sport. This time it was for middle-aged businessmen to play during their lunch hour at the YMCA. Learn more about its origins; its inventor, William G. Morgan; and how basketball influenced the sport at the International Volleyball Hall of Fame.

The nonprofit organization is dedicated to preserving and telling the history of volleyball, as well as honoring the players. The museum has hundreds of historical volleyball artifacts displayed, with timelines, and other memorabilia. It is perhaps best known, though, for its annual Induction Celebration honoring the sport's elite, with 160 inductees from 25 countries.

444 Dwight St., Holyoke, 413-536-0926
usavolleyball.org/hall-of-fame

HANG AROUND
THE HERITAGE MUSEUMS & GARDENS

Founded in 1969, this property is the largest public garden in southern New England, with 100 acres to explore and a variety of exhibits, including a collection of classic cars, American decorative and folk art, and traveling exhibits spread out over three buildings. The varieties of trees, shrubs, and flowers number in the thousands. Other highlights at the museum include a windmill, built in Orleans, Massachusetts, in 1800; a working vintage 1912 carousel; a labyrinth; and Hidden Hollow, a two-acre playground for children under age 10.

The property hosts lots of events centered around what's in bloom. In May and June, the gardens' impressive collection of rhododendrons, which number in the tens of thousands, are not to be missed. In July, it's the hydrangeas' turn. The Daylily Garden is especially spectacular in the summer. There are several miles of nature trails, too, plus an Adventure Park, with zip lines and climbing challenges.

67 Grove St., Sandwich, 508-888-3300
heritagemuseumsandgardens.org

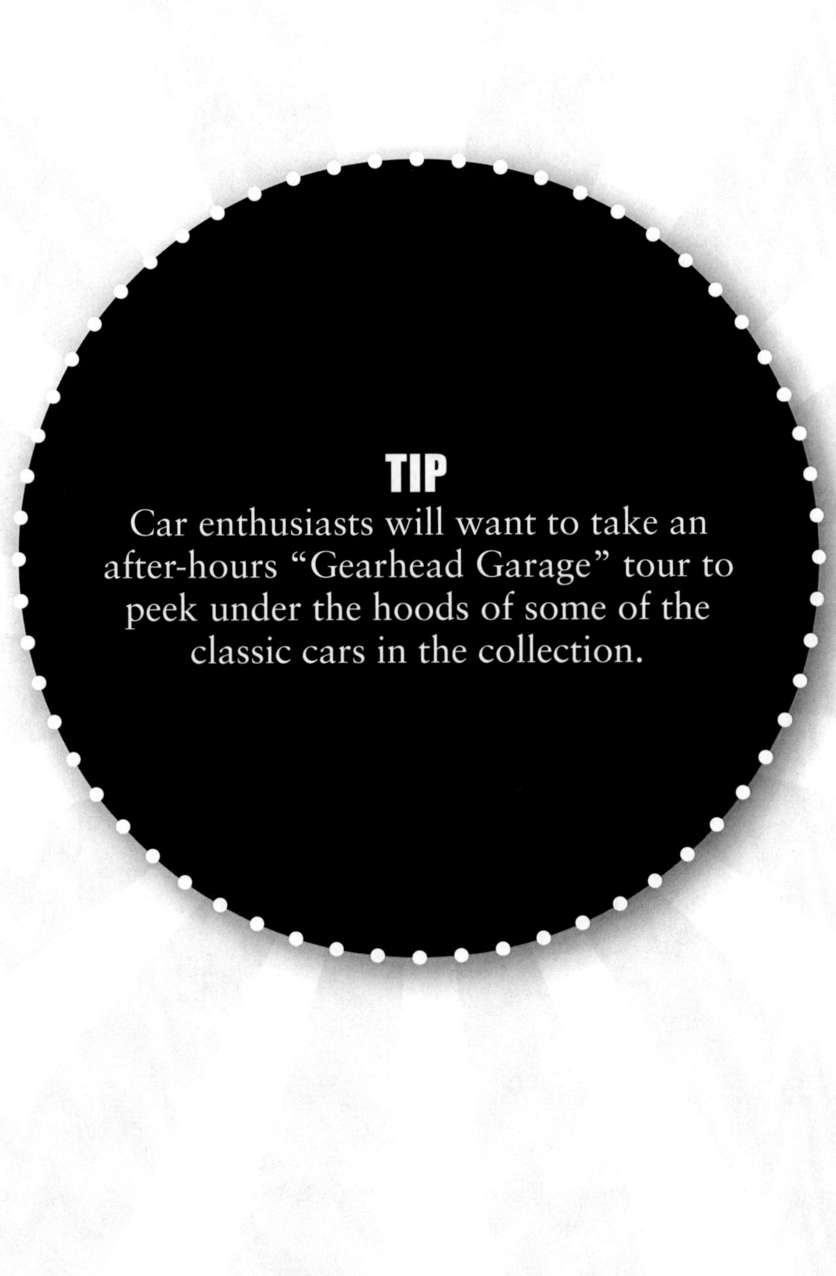
TIP
Car enthusiasts will want to take an after-hours "Gearhead Garage" tour to peek under the hoods of some of the classic cars in the collection.

60

CHEER ON THE BOYS OF SUMMER ON CAPE COD

The Cape Cod Baseball League officially formed in 1923 but has roots dating back to 1885, and it's the premier collegiate summer baseball league in the nation. Players from across the country, representing all NCAA college divisions, are recruited to play in the 10-team wooden bat league. If you are vacationing on the Cape, watching a game is a fantastic summer pastime.

The league plays from mid-June to mid-August, with a 44-game regular-season schedule and a postseason made up of best-of-three quarterfinal, semifinal, and championship series. Teams are located in Bourne, Brewster, Chatham, Cotuit, Falmouth, Harwich, Hyannis, Orleans, Wareham, and Yarmouth-Dennis, and games rotate through the towns. More than a thousand major league players have been in the league, so you are sure to see a good game!

capecodleague.com

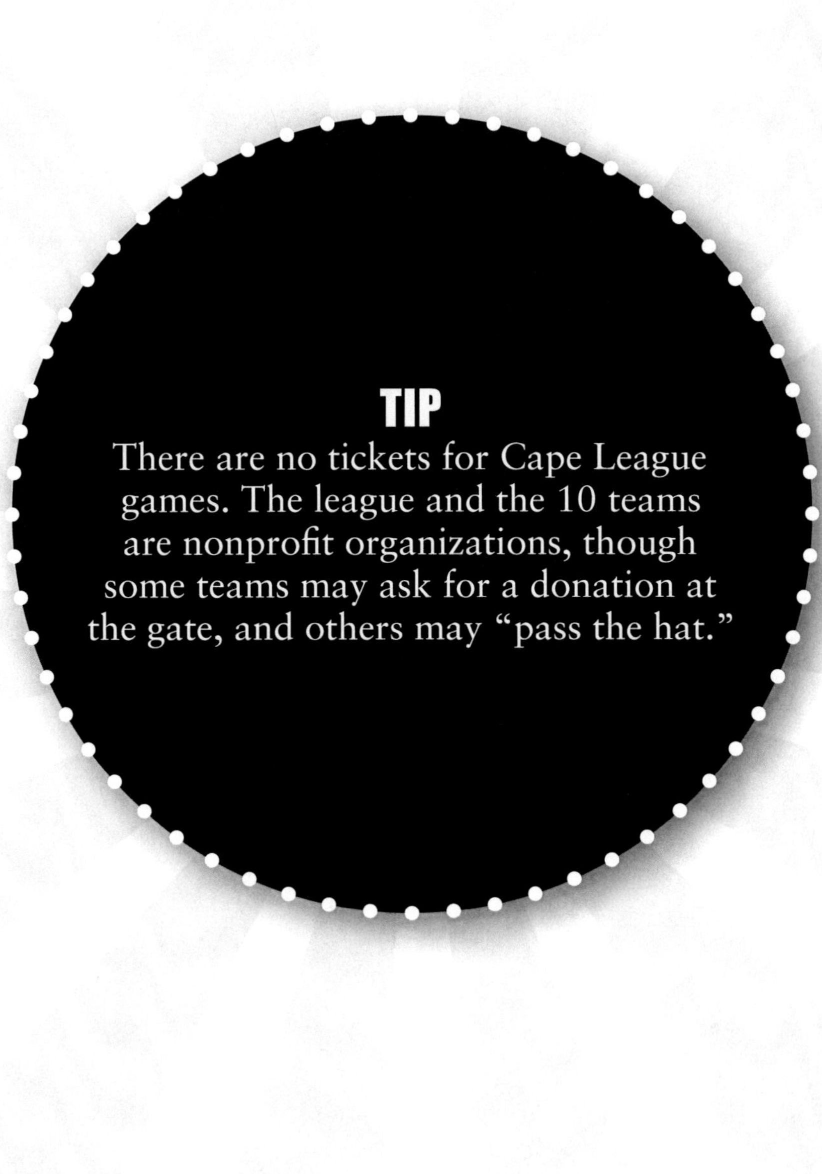
TIP
There are no tickets for Cape League games. The league and the 10 teams are nonprofit organizations, though some teams may ask for a donation at the gate, and others may "pass the hat."

61

TREK
THE CAPE COD RAIL TRAIL

This 25-mile paved trail on a former railroad right-of-way offers an escape from the Cape's notorious vehicle traffic. It passes through Dennis, Harwich, Brewster, Orleans, Eastham, and Wellfleet. Happily, the trail is pretty flat and can accommodate everyone, including horseback riders, walkers, and runners. You can easily detour to visit beaches and lighthouses, or to get a snack or a drink along the way.

The railroad tracks date back to 1848, when the Old Colony Railroad Company ran between Boston and Sandwich. As cars replaced trains in popularity, the service was ended, and for years the tracks were ignored and neglected, but you'd never know that today. It's easy to jump on the trail from any number of places, but if you need to park a car, you can leave it at the Salt Pond Visitor Center in Eastham, which is open year-round.

50 Nauset Rd., Eastham, 508-896-3491
mass.gov/locations/cape-cod-rail-trail

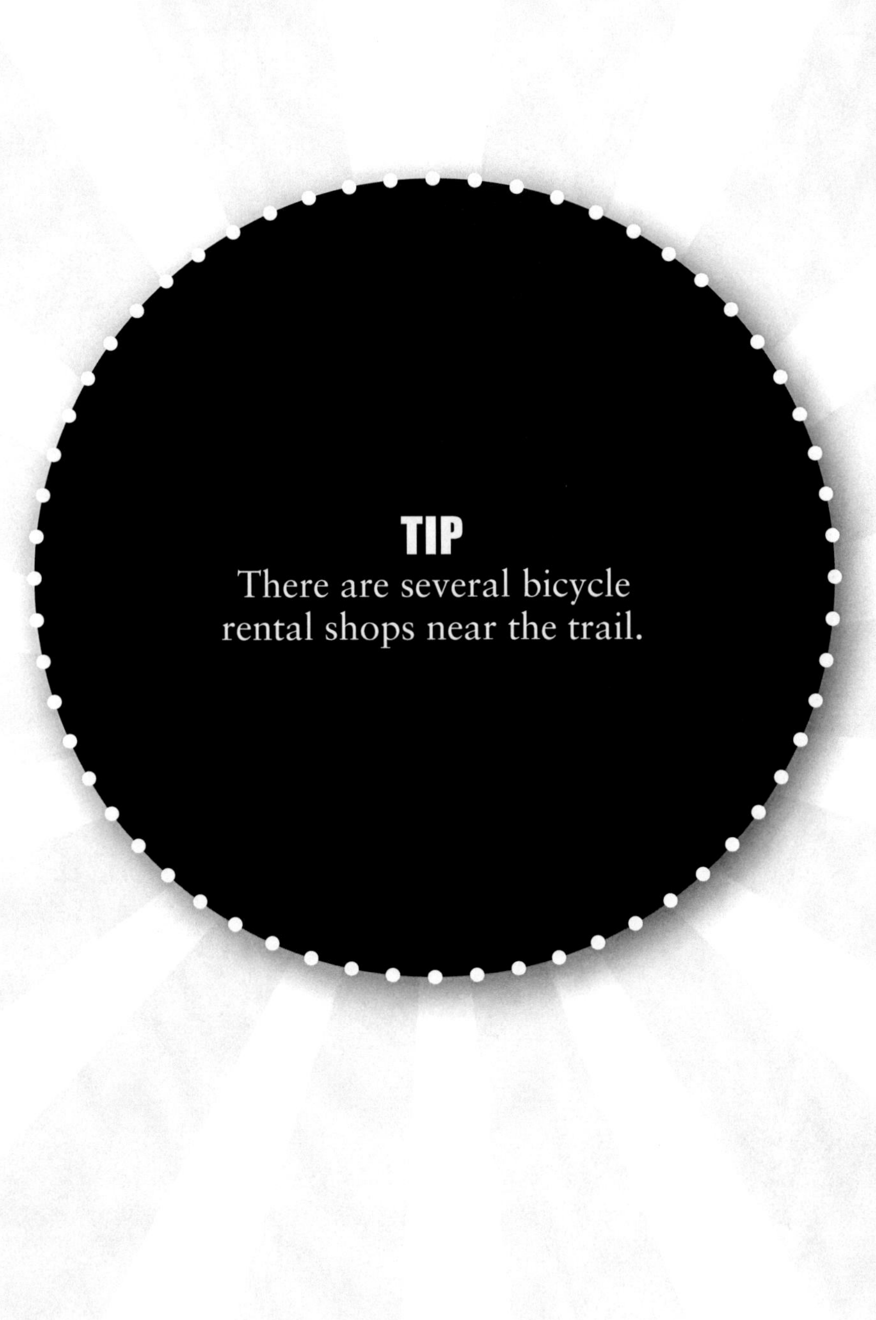

TIP

There are several bicycle rental shops near the trail.

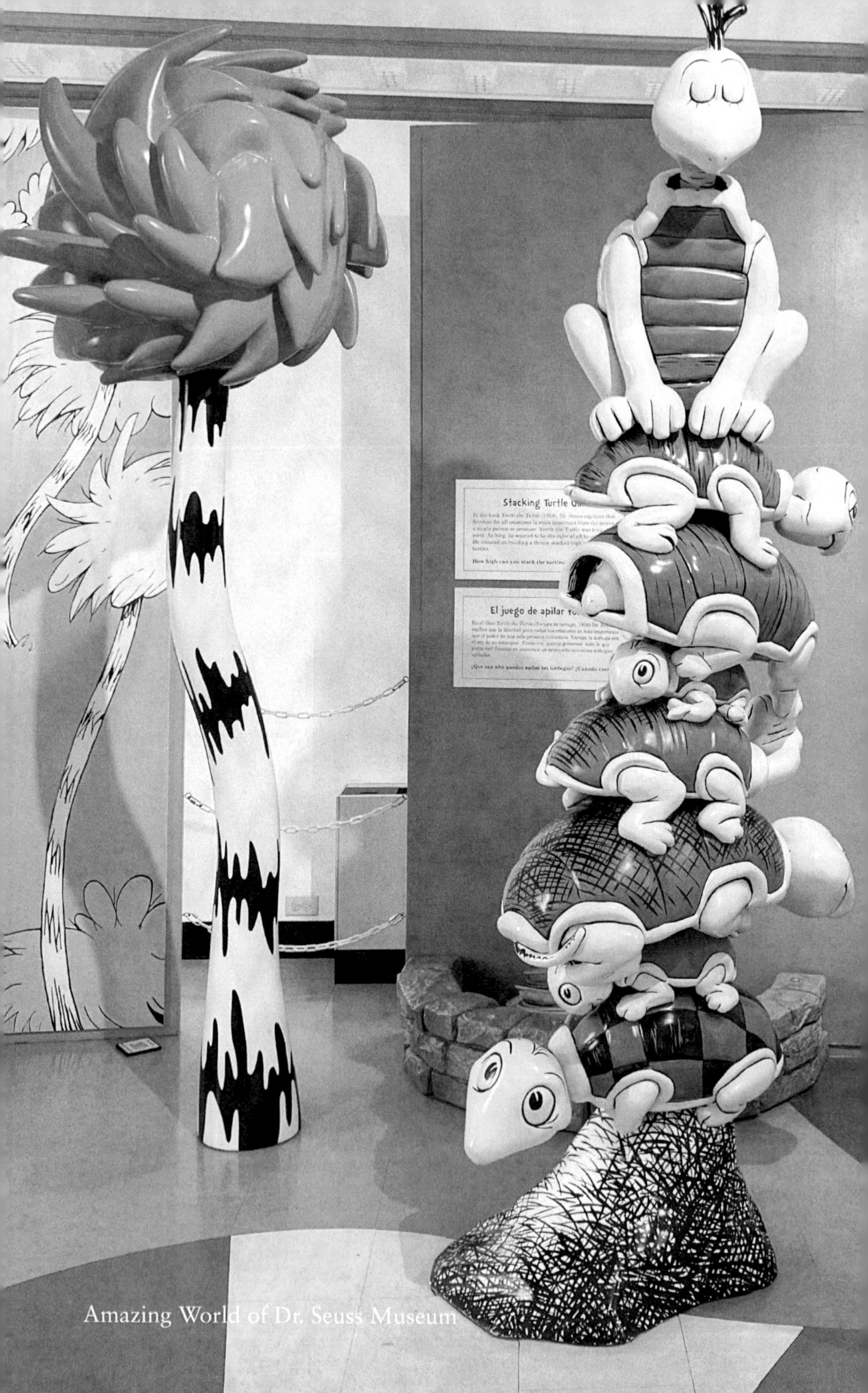

Amazing World of Dr. Seuss Museum

CULTURE AND HISTORY

TRAVEL BACK IN TIME
ON THE FREEDOM TRAIL

The Freedom Trail is probably the most famous attraction in Boston and a fantastic way to learn about many of the city's significant contributions to the American Revolutionary War. The 2.5-mile trail leads you to 16 sites, including Faneuil Hall, Old North Church, the Paul Revere House, King's Chapel, and the Bunker Hill Monument. There are plenty of places to stop along the route to eat, drink, or just rest your feet.

A little-known fact about how the trail came to be is a fun story. In 1951, a columnist for a local paper wrote that there should be markers for people to find the various sites around town. "All I'm suggesting is that we mark out a 'Puritan Path' or 'Liberty Loop' or 'Freedom's Way' or whatever you want to call it, so [visitors and locals will] know where to start and what course to follow." In short order, the mayor agreed, and the first iteration of the trail began!

Boston Common Visitor Information Center
139 Tremont St., Boston, 617-357-8300
thefreedomtrail.org

MORE BOSTON TRAILS

Several other themed trails in Boston offer different perspectives and highlight important historic milestones and people who have shaped the city.

Black Heritage Trail

The Black Heritage Trail is a 1.6-mile trail of 10 sites throughout Beacon Hill, with stops like the 54th Regiment Memorial, the Abiel Smith School, and the African Meeting House.

nps.gov/thingstodo/black-heritage-trail-tour.htm

Irish Heritage Trail

Learn about Irish American sculptors, poets, veterans, and politicians who have had an impact in Boston, such as John F. Kennedy and James Michael Curley, with 20 stops from the Fens to Faneuil Hall.

irishheritagetrail.com

Women's Heritage Trail

The Women's Heritage Trail tells the stories of women, from patriots to intellectuals, from abolitionists to suffragists, and from writers to artists, of the past four centuries.

bwht.org

TOSS SOME TEA
AT THE BOSTON TEA PARTY SHIPS & MUSEUM

The Boston Tea Party Ships & Museum is a wonderfully hands-on, interactive venue, where you can throw (fake) tea overboard, climb around replicas of the brigs *Beaver* and *Eleanor* (two of the three ships involved in the Boston Tea Party), and chat with period actors about colonial issues. Your visit starts with a greeting from Samuel Adams laying out the facts of what's at stake in 1773.

Exhibits at the museum, which is located on Griffin's Wharf, close to where the actual Tea Party occurred on December 16, 1773, include cool 3D holograms, talking portraits, and the Robinson Tea Chest, one of two original tea chests known to exist. In the panoramic Minuteman Theater, you can watch a powerful film, called *Let It Begin Here*, which makes you feel like you are part of the action on April 19, 1775, including Paul Revere's famous "Midnight Ride."

306 Congress St., Boston, 866-955-0667
bostonteapartyship.com

TIP
Take time for tea in Abigail's Tea Room,
which has one of the best views of the harbor
around, as well as delicious scones.

MAKE A DAY OF IT
AT THE MFA

Home to more than half a million objects ranging from ancient Greek and Roman artifacts to modern photography, the world-class Museum of Fine Arts, Boston, is worth at least a full day of your time, if not more. It can feel overwhelming to know where to begin, so it's smart to make a game plan in advance.

The Art of the Americas wing is a great place to start, with 16,000 objects spanning 3,000 years. The wing includes highlights such as early colonial New England decorative arts and paintings, with John Singleton Copley's famous portrait of Paul Revere and the silversmith's Sons of Liberty Bowl. The Art of Ancient Egypt galleries boast 65,000 works, while the Contemporary Art collection features work from the second half of the 20th century to the present day. And of course, there is a lovely restaurant and a café.

465 Huntington Ave., Boston, 617-267-9300
mfa.org

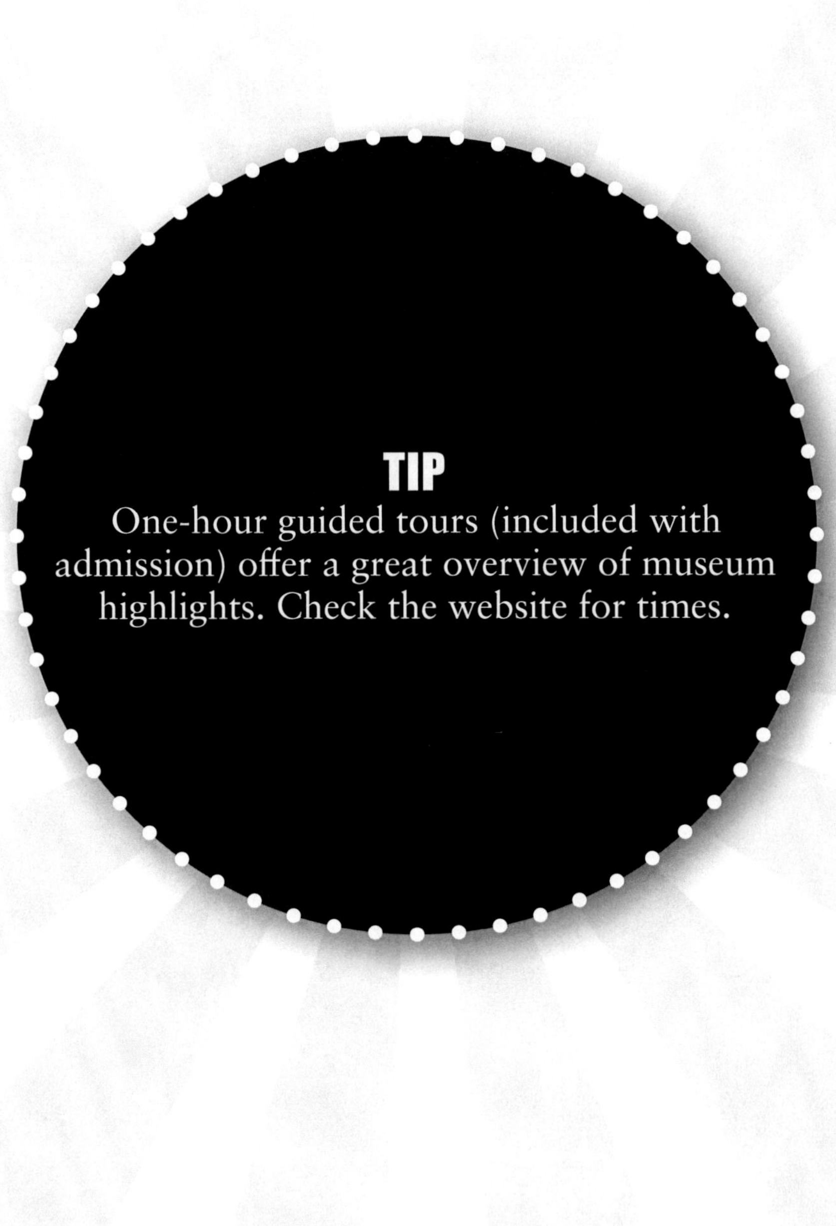
TIP
One-hour guided tours (included with admission) offer a great overview of museum highlights. Check the website for times.

CHECK OUT
THE BOSTON PUBLIC LIBRARY

You don't need a library card to visit the main branch of Boston's library system in Copley Square, or even to check out a book. Our nation's first free library began circulating books in 1854 and is now located in a magnificent 1895 Renaissance Beaux-Arts Classicism building. Besides books, it's home to world-class artworks and murals, as well as the stunning 218-foot-long reading room with a 50-foot-high barrel-arch ceiling. At the main entrance, you'll see immense stone lions crafted by Louis Saint-Gaudens, a grand marble staircase, and murals painted by French artist Pierre Puvis de Chavannes depicting the nine muses. Upstairs, there's John Singer Sargent's mural series, the *Triumph of Religion*. Don't miss the beautiful Renaissance-style courtyard, which is an exact replica of the one in Rome's Palazzo della Cancelleria. Free art and architecture tours are also offered.

700 Boylston St., Boston, 617-536-5400
bpl.org

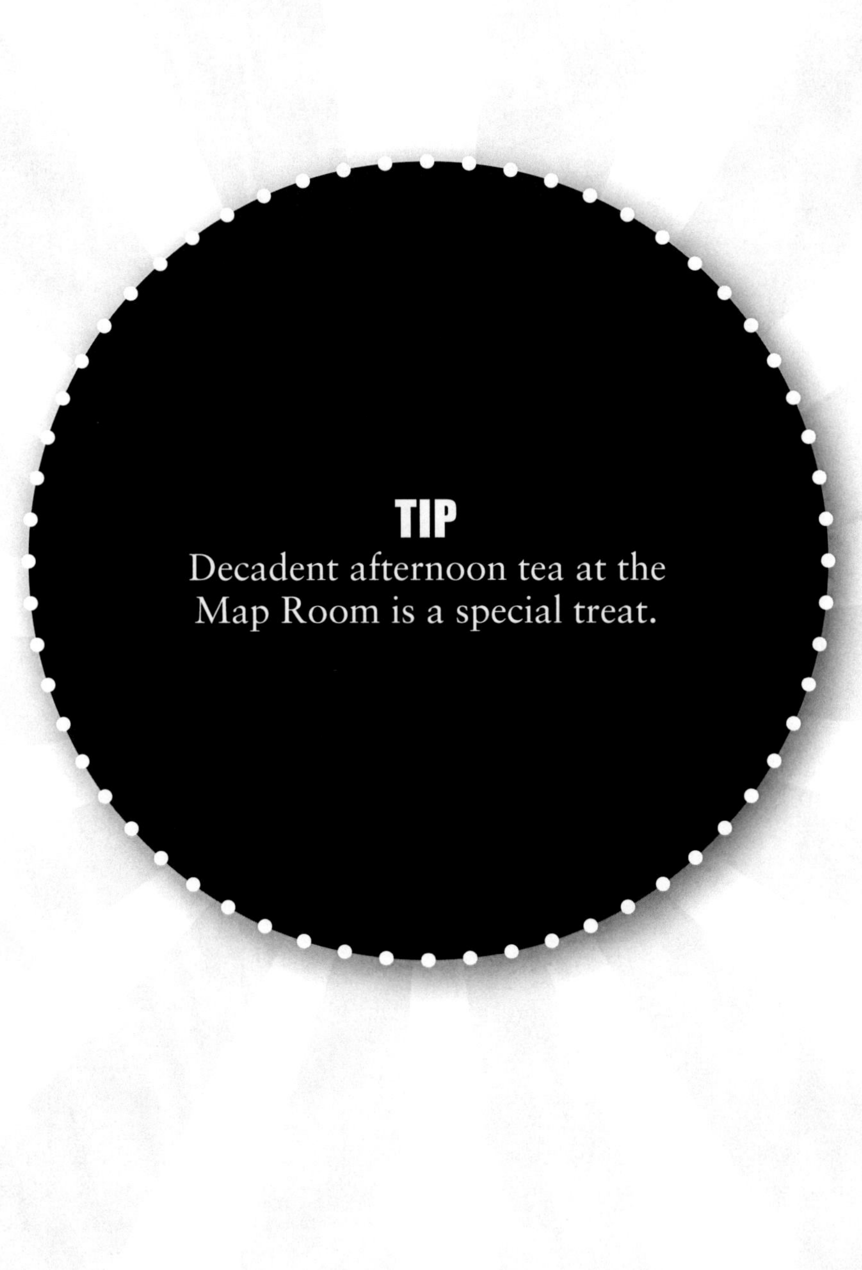
TIP
Decadent afternoon tea at the Map Room is a special treat.

GO EDGY
AT THE ICA

From the time the Institute of Contemporary Art was founded in 1936, it's been instrumental in identifying and showcasing the most important artists of the day, such as Andy Warhol, Edvard Munch, Laurie Anderson, and Roy Lichtenstein. The stunning glass-walled cantilevered museum on the Boston waterfront in the Seaport District opened in 2006 and helped invigorate the neighborhood. It offers breathtaking views both inside and out.

There is always something new going on at the ICA, with ever-changing exhibitions, live music and dance performances, provocative film and digital media selections, talks, tours, family activities, and teen programming. You can also hop on a free water shuttle to zip over to the ICA Watershed, a seasonal exhibition space in East Boston. The museum's First Friday series in the summer is always lively and fun, featuring anything from guest DJs to pop-up installations.

25 Harbor Shore Dr., Boston, 617-478-3100
icaboston.org

TIP

On Thursdays after 5 p.m., admission is free.

EXPLORE
OLD NORTH CHURCH

Visit the very spot where Paul Revere and the sexton Robert Newman managed to signal the departure by water of the British regulars to Lexington and Concord on the night of April 18, 1775. Old North Church, built in 1723, is Boston's oldest standing church building, and to this day it has an active Episcopal congregation where visitors are welcome for services.

You can also take a Behind the Scenes tour and visit the bell-ringing chamber and the crypt. You will head up the same stairs Paul Revere trod upon at that pivotal moment. Inside the church, you can sit in a box pew (when there are no services) and listen to a short presentation about the founding of Old North, the lantern story, and the church's role in the American Revolution. Down below in the crypt, 37 tombs serve as the final resting place of 1,100 people, the most famous of whom is Samuel Nicholson, the first captain of the USS *Constitution*.

193 Salem St., Boston, 617-858-8231
oldnorth.com

ENJOY THE INTIMATE ISABELLA STEWART GARDNER MUSEUM

A beloved Boston grande dame, Isabella Stewart came to the city from New York to marry John Lowell Gardner, one of Boston's leading citizens, in 1860. Her grandest project and enduring legacy is the stunning Venetian palazzo she had built to display her exquisite collection of art, mainly from Europe. Now a museum, the collection includes Titian's *Rape of Europa*, Giotto's *Presentation of Christ Child in the Temple*, and John Singer Sargent's *El Jaleo*, among others. The indoor courtyard is magnificent year-round, with 10 seasonal floral displays.

As stipulated in her will, the intimate museum is exactly as she left it, and it feels like she might pop in at any moment, though there are a couple of notable changes. In 1990, 13 pieces of priceless artwork were stolen and are still missing to this day. An addition was also built in 2012, with a music hall, exhibit space, and conservation labs.

25 Evans Way, Boston, 617-566-1401
gardnermuseum.org

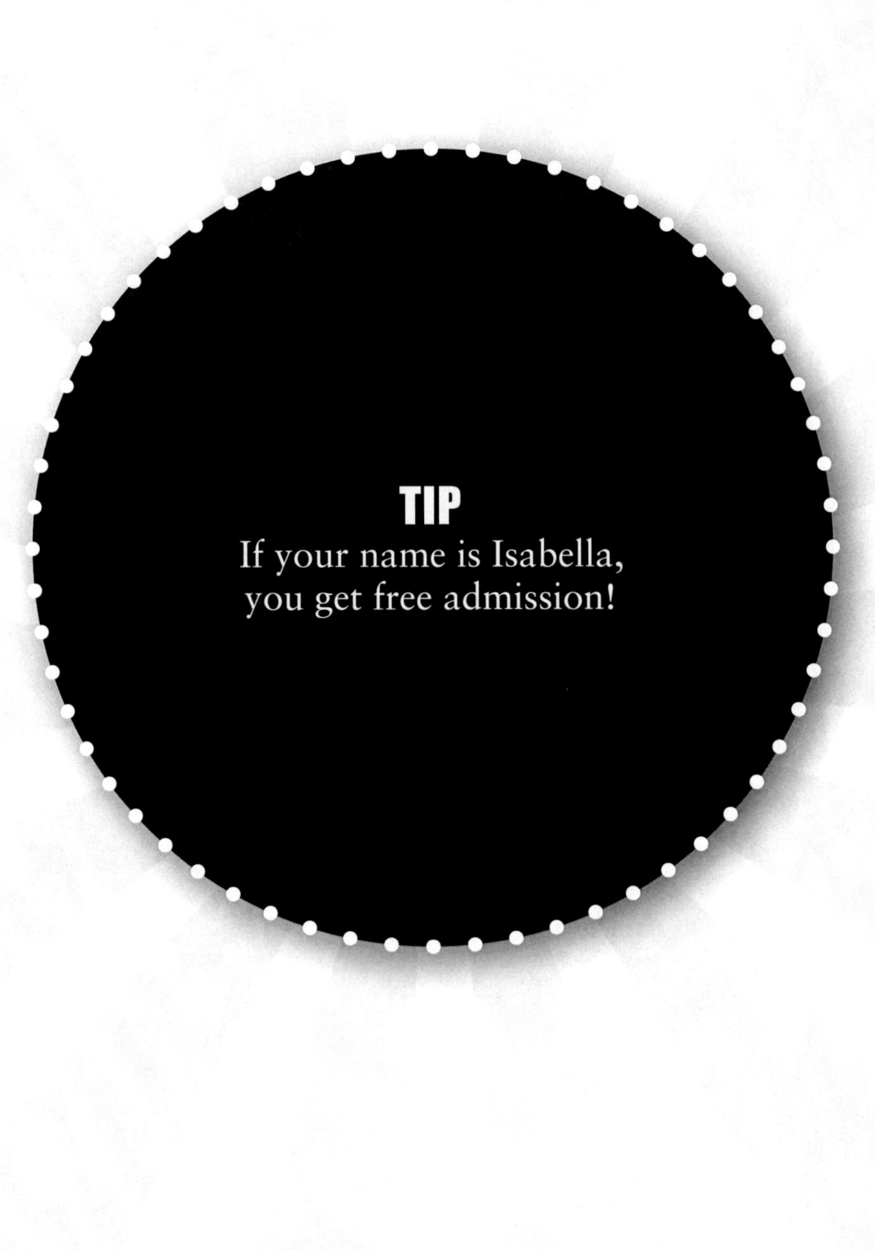
TIP
If your name is Isabella,
you get free admission!

HANG OUT
IN HARVARD SQUARE

Harvard Square, home to Harvard University, is the unofficial "capital" of Cambridge. It's packed with boutiques, bookstores, cool art houses, and great cafés and restaurants perfect for people watching. Start with a visit to Harvard University, the nation's oldest institution of higher education. Enter through one of its many gates and wander the Old Yard at your leisure, or sign up for a free tour, where student guides will tell you about the campus.

As one might expect, Harvard has world-class museums to visit, too, including the Natural History, Archaeology & Ethnology, Ancient Near East, and Art museums, among others. Whatever else you do, don't miss the magical Ware Collection of Blaschka Glass Models of Plants, better known as the "Glass Flowers." Make a stop at the Harvard Book Store and grab a souvenir T-shirt and simply walk around the neighborhood, taking in the historic homes.

Cambridge, 617-495-1000
harvardsquare.com

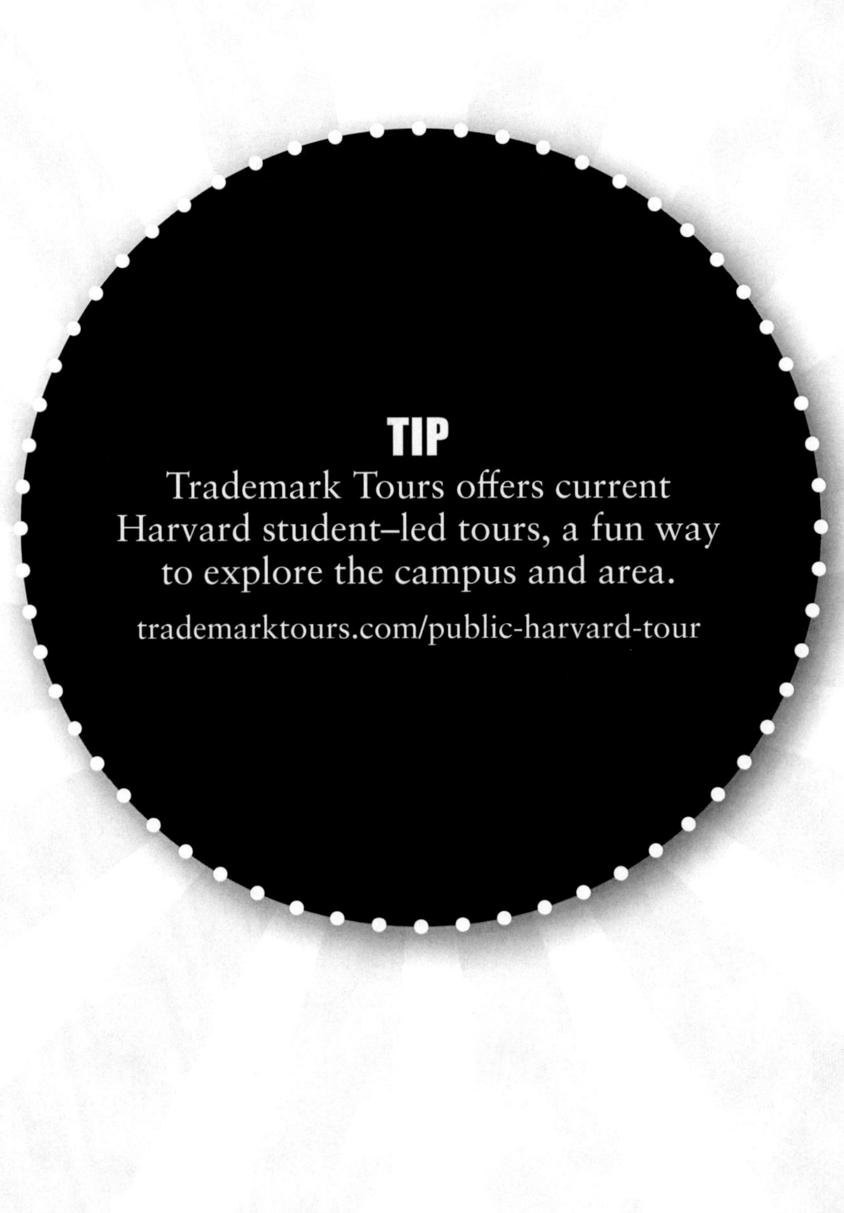
TIP
Trademark Tours offers current Harvard student–led tours, a fun way to explore the campus and area.
trademarktours.com/public-harvard-tour

PERUSE
THE PEABODY ESSEX MUSEUM

The oldest continuously operating museum in the country has a collection of more than 850,000 works from around the globe reflecting the wealth that shipping brought to Salem. The collections include American art and architecture, Asian art, photography, and maritime art and history, as well as Native American, Oceanic, and African art. One exhibit you shouldn't miss is the Yin Yu Tang house, a 200-year-old house dating to the Qing Dynasty (1644–1911) that the museum brought over from China in sections and reassembled. An excellent one-hour self-guided audio tour offers a highlight of 21 objects throughout the museum.

In addition to the main museum, PEM, as it is known, has other places to explore in its three-block campus, including the 5,000-square-foot Museum Garden and the Colonial Revival Ropes Mansion Garden. The historic Ropes Mansion, built in the 1700s, is open on certain weekends for self-guided tours, too.

161 Essex St., Salem, 978-745-9500
pem.org

STEP BACK IN TIME
AT OLD STURBRIDGE VILLAGE

This 240-acre attraction is the Northeast's largest outdoor history museum and depicts a rural New England town of the early 19th century, allowing visitors to imagine life in the 1830s. There are more than 40 historic buildings to explore, including houses, farms, trade shops, meetinghouses, a district school, and a country store, among others.

The museum is organized into the Center Village and Countryside. The Village has a grassy common surrounded by homes, trade shops, and businesses. In the Countryside, there are also homes, plus working farms, trade shops, a mill pond with three water-powered mills, and an exhibit gallery. As you wander the grounds, you can see live demos, take part in hands-on crafts, see heritage animals, listen to period music or lectures, and much more. You can easily make a full day of visiting and take a break at one of two cafés or the bake shop, plus shop at the Ox & Yoke Mercantile for village-artisan-made wares.

1 Old Sturbridge Village Rd., Sturbridge, 800-733-1830
osv.org

IMMERSE YOURSELF
IN AMERICAN HISTORY

From the sites of the first skirmishes of the Revolutionary War to the homes of some of the country's early important authors, Concord and Lexington offer a lot to see and do. And besides all the rich history, both are beautiful examples of picture-perfect New England towns. You can hit most of the signature spots on a day trip and still have time to relax and dine in one of the many charming cafés or restaurants in both towns.

Start at the excellent Lexington Visitors Center, where you can see interactive exhibits, pick up maps, and sign up for walking tours. Just outside are the Lexington Battle Green, Buckman Tavern, Hancock-Clarke House, and other important Revolutionary sites. Then you can head over to Concord, first to the North Bridge, where the "shot heard round the world" happened, then take time at the Wayside, where Nathaniel Hawthorne, Louisa May Alcott, and Margaret Sidney (Harriett Lothrop) lived at one time or another.

Lexington Visitors Center
1875 Massachusetts Ave., Lexington, 781-862-1450
tourlexington.us/visitors-center

Concord Visitors Center
58 Main St., Concord, 978-318-3061
visitconcord.org/visit/visitor-center

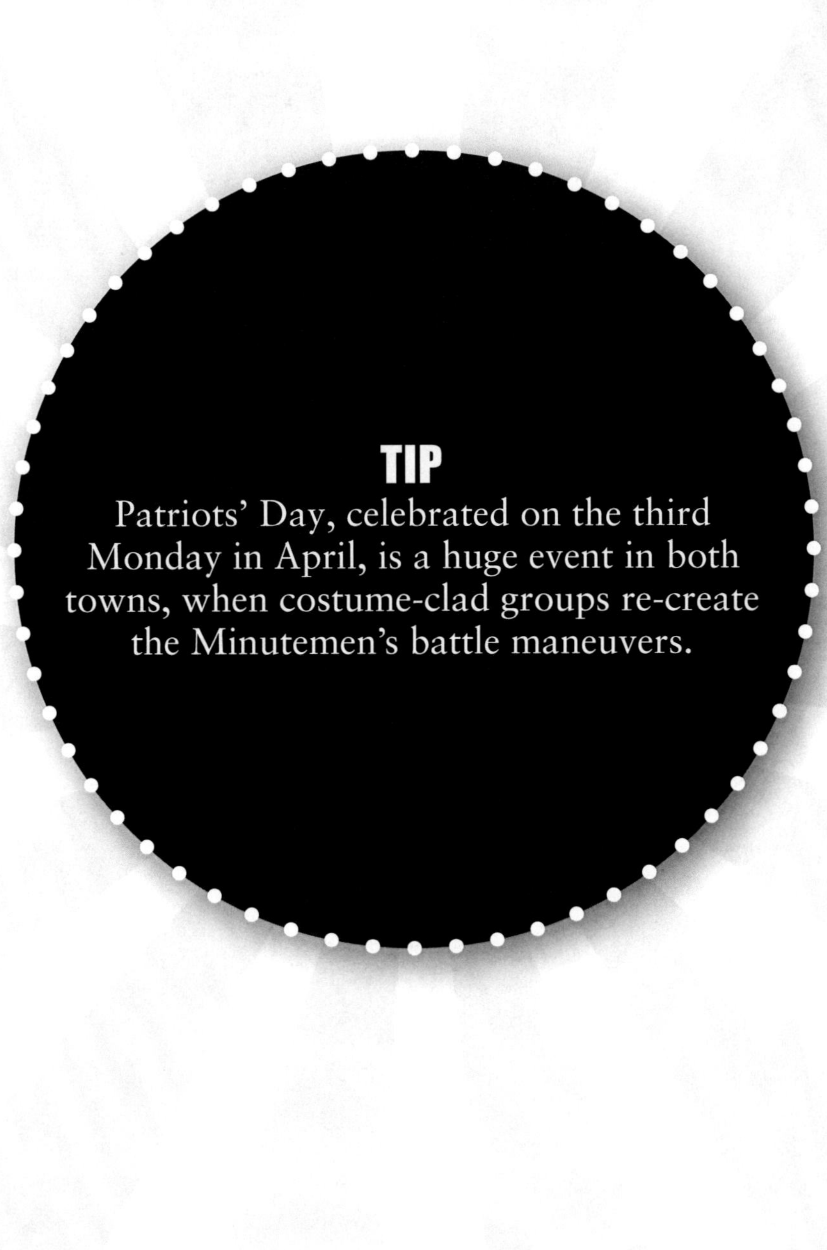

TIP

Patriots' Day, celebrated on the third Monday in April, is a huge event in both towns, when costume-clad groups re-create the Minutemen's battle maneuvers.

PAY A VISIT
TO THE PLIMOTH PATUXET MUSEUMS

For an authentic and honest look at what life was like in the 1620s, visit this living history museum, which tells the interwoven story of the Plymouth Colony Pilgrims and the Wampanoag tribal homeland with integrity. Main exhibits include the Historic Patuxet Homesite, the 17th-Century English Village, and the *Mayflower II*.

At the re-created village, you'll encounter thatched-roof homes, reproductions of items the Pilgrims might have used, heritage breeds of livestock, and "residents," who never break out of character. They will chat with you and answer questions about the 1600s, but there are also interpreters who can help with modern questions. On the Wampanoag homesite, meet native people who provide a perspective on the traditions, lifeways, and culture of the Eastern Woodlands Indigenous people, who have lived here for more than 12,000 years.

137 Warren Ave., Plymouth, 508-746-1622
plimoth.org

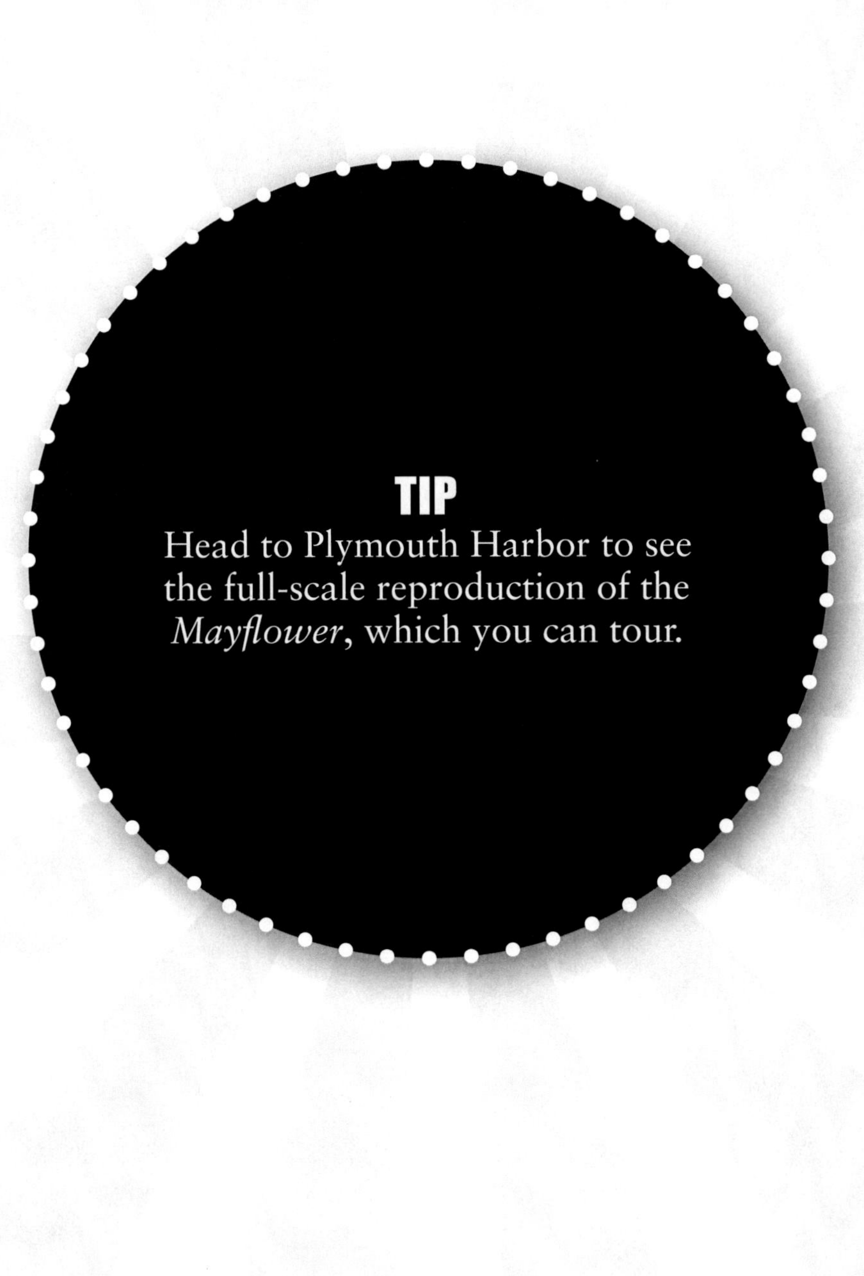
TIP
Head to Plymouth Harbor to see the full-scale reproduction of the *Mayflower*, which you can tour.

MEANDER
THROUGH MASS MOCA

The Massachusetts Museum of Contemporary Art, or MASS MoCA, features enormous galleries in a former factory with 250,000 square feet of space, which means the museum can allow artists to stage impressive large-scale, immersive installations. There are a mix of permanent and temporary exhibits. A highlight is the Sol LeWitt: A Wall Drawing Retrospective, which boasts 105 of the artist's large-scale wall drawings, occupying nearly an acre of interior walls installed over three stories of a historic mill building. Other featured artists include Laurie Anderson, John Cage, and James Turrell.

Besides artwork and installations, the museum is a vibrant hub of everything from music to film to theater. More than 75 performances are offered year-round, including concerts (I saw Blondie there!), contemporary dance, cabaret, dance parties, indie rock, progressive bluegrass, outdoor silent films with live music, documentaries, and avant-garde theater.

1040 Mass MoCA Way, North Adams, 413-662-2111
massmoca.org

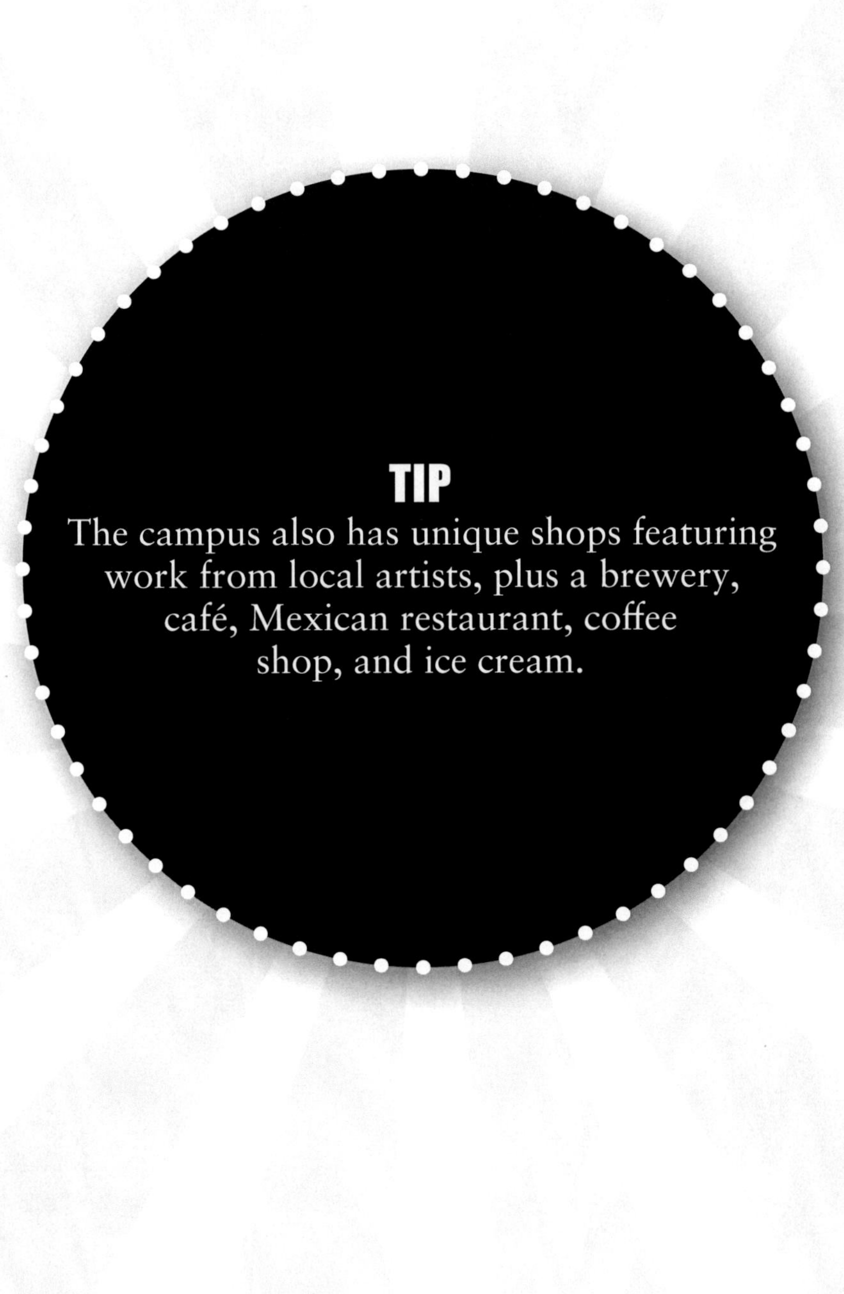
TIP
The campus also has unique shops featuring work from local artists, plus a brewery, café, Mexican restaurant, coffee shop, and ice cream.

SINK INTO SALEM'S HISTORY

For better or worse, Salem is synonymous with witches. Despite this dark chapter in American history, the city now embraces all things witchy. For sure, you can learn all about the notorious 1692 witch trials at sites like the Witch House and the Salem Witch Museum, but you can also enjoy whimsically themed souvenir shops and an entire month of Halloween fun in October.

There are plenty of other things to see and do in the coastal town, from learning about its seafaring history at the Salem Maritime National Historic Site to visiting the House of the Seven Gables, home of writer Nathaniel Hawthorne. The Salem Trolley offers one-hour guided tours of the city, a great way to get an introduction to the town. And be sure to get to the Essex Street Pedestrian Mall, a bustling hub of activity, with boutiques, cafés, bars, shops, galleries, and museums.

Destination Salem Visitor Information Center
245 Derby St., Salem, 978-741-3252
salem.org

LEARN ABOUT
LOWELL

During the Industrial Revolution, Lowell was a major hub of the Massachusetts textile industry, which supplied the entire country. The city's first mill opened in 1823, and by the 1850s, there were 40 factories employing thousands of workers, the majority of whom were immigrants and unmarried young women known as "Mill Girls." Life was definitely no carousel for these workers.

Today, the Lowell National Historical Park features exhibits about everything from workers' lives to the equipment they used and how the waterways played a vital role. The Boott Cotton Mills Museum, a park highlight, re-creates the look and atmosphere of a textile factory floor with more than 80 historic power looms from the 1920s. Visitors can experience a fraction of what Lowell's mill girls and immigrant laborers would have seen, heard, smelled, and felt. The park offers a variety of guided tours, which are a great way to learn about the history and area in more depth.

246 Market St., Lowell, 978-458-8750
nps.gov/lowe/planyourvisit/index.htm

BENEFIT FROM A BUNDLE
AT SPRINGFIELD MUSEUMS

Plan accordingly and make the most of the great deal that the Springfield Museums offer: access to five museums for one admission price. Your single ticket includes the Amazing World of Dr. Seuss Museum (and the Dr. Seuss National Memorial Sculpture Garden), the Springfield Science Museum, the Michele and Donald D'Amour Museum of Fine Arts, the Lyman and Merrie Wood Museum of Springfield History, and the George Walter Vincent Smith Art Museum. The museums are located downtown in a quadrangle, so visiting them all is easy.

Whether you want to learn about the life and times of Theodor Seuss Geisel, check out a life-size replica of a Tyrannosaurus rex, enjoy 18th-century French art, peruse the largest collection of Indian Motorcycle bikes and memorabilia in the world, or see one of the largest collections of Chinese cloisonné outside of Asia, this is the place! And this barely touches what you can see across the five outstanding museums.

21 Edwards St., Springfield, 413-263-6800
springfieldmuseums.org

GET DRAWN INTO
THE NORMAN ROCKWELL MUSEUM

Dedicated to the beloved artist who painted small-town American life with care and insight, the Norman Rockwell Museum, located in Stockbridge, is home to the world's largest and most significant collection of Rockwell's work. Rockwell spent the last 25 years of his life in the town, and he and his wife helped found the museum in 1969.

The museum, set on 36 acres in the Berkshires, holds 998 of his original paintings and drawings, all 323 of his *Saturday Evening Post* covers, advertisements, and more from the prolific artist. Certainly, the breadth of Rockwell's work is amazing. Visitors can also see his studio, which was relocated to the museum grounds and includes his original art materials, library, and furnishings. Temporary exhibits, such as a recent one about the art of *Mad* magazine, offer a look at different artists, themes, and current trends in illustration.

9 Glendale Rd., Stockbridge, 413-298-4100
nrm.org

ENCOUNTER 51 CENTURIES OF ART
AT THE WORCESTER ART MUSEUM

You can't exactly put a label on the Worcester Art Museum, which was founded in 1896 and boasts a 38,000-piece collection covering 51 centuries of art. How many museums can list a 12th-century medieval chapter house, which was moved from France and rebuilt stone by stone inside the museum; works from Andy Warhol; and paintings by Winslow Homer under the same roof? The museum is wonderfully eclectic, so whether you are interested in photography, American folk art, or ancient art from Greece, there is something for everyone.

The museum is also home to the second-largest collection of arms and armor in the United States, with more than 1,500 objects, with origins ranging from ancient Egypt to 19th-century Japan. Of note are the full suits of armor from around the world. The collection offers hands-on events, such as trying on armor and live demonstrations of swordplay or armored combat, which are lots of fun. Themed tours, artist talks, and other events are offered, too.

55 Salisbury St., Worcester, 508-799-4406
worcesterart.org

BE WOWED
AT THE NEW BEDFORD WHALING MUSEUM

The New Bedford Whaling Museum offers a comprehensive look at the history, culture, science, and art of this region of Massachusetts and the whaling industry throughout the centuries. Most whaling voyages from New Bedford stopped in the Portuguese Atlantic Islands of the Azores and Cape Verde, which had a huge impact on the town's population and culture, with waves of immigrants coming to make their home in New Bedford.

The permanent exhibit Whales Today provides an introduction to whale biology and whale conservation; "Cultures of Whaling" describes places where whale hunting was significant and why; and "Lagoda" is a half-scale model of a whaling bark that was built inside the building in 1916. Another highlight at the museum is its impressive Scrimshaw Gallery, which sports the largest collection of scrimshaw in the world. Join a free guided tour for an overview of all the exhibits, including the museum's five whale skeletons.

18 Johnny Cake Hill, New Bedford, 508-997-0046
whalingmuseum.org

TOUR THE GROUNDS
OF THE DECORDOVA SCULPTURE PARK AND MUSEUM

While the indoor part of the deCordova museum is undergoing renovations to upgrade some of its systems (probably into late 2025 or 2026), visitors can still visit the park's grounds, where more than 60 site-specific, large-scale works of art can be seen. Permanent and temporary sculptures are installed among 30 acres of lawns, forests, fields, gardens, and terraces along the shore of Flint's Pond. Besides enjoying the sculptures, visitors can participate in activities such as curator and artist conversations, yoga, nature tours, and special talks and screenings.

When the museum does reopen, visitors will once again have access to a large collection of works by artists with deep connections to the New England region dating from 1950, which the museum specializes in. The permanent collection is particularly heavy on photography, with more than 1,500 artworks. The museum shop and café remain open through the renovations.

51 Sandy Pond Rd., Lincoln, 781-259-8355
thetrustees.org/place/decordova

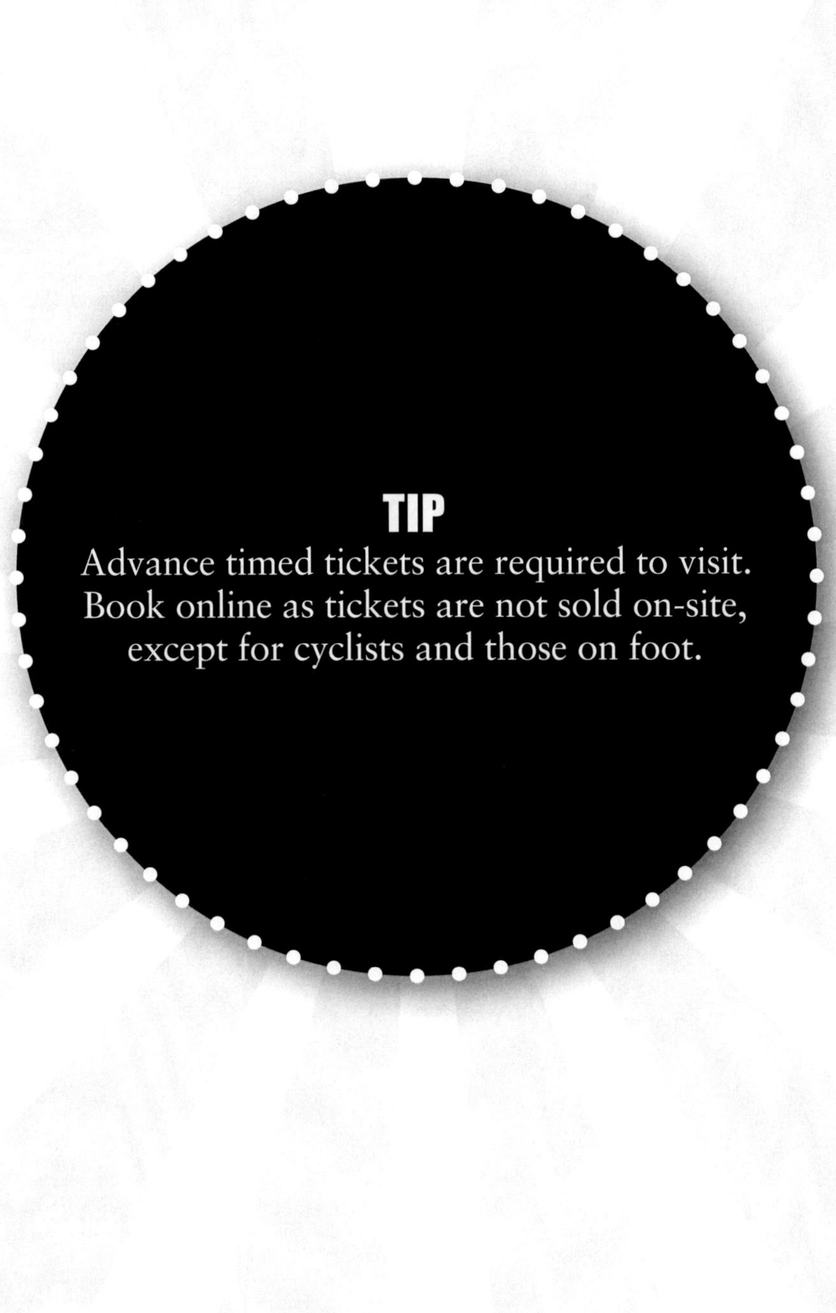
TIP
Advance timed tickets are required to visit.
Book online as tickets are not sold on-site,
except for cyclists and those on foot.

MAKE IT
TO MARTHA'S VINEYARD

Martha's Vineyard, seven miles off the coast, is about 100 square miles in size with six distinct towns. Besides its many beaches and five lighthouses, each of the island's towns has its own charms and character, making it fun to compare and contrast. If you arrive by the 45-minute ferry into the towns of Oak Bluffs or Vineyard Haven without a car, you can easily rent one, as well as mopeds or bicycles. The island also has a very efficient bus system.

Oak Bluffs is famous for its 300 tiny, colorful "gingerbread" houses, originally built by 19th-century Methodists who came to the Vineyard to worship, first staying in temporary quarters, then later in these tiny houses. Vineyard Haven is a cultural district, with historic sites and attractions. Edgartown is famous for its 18th-century whaling captains' mansions; Aquinnah for its stunning clay cliffs and the Gay Head Lighthouse; Chilmark, with quiet fishing villages; and West Tisbury, with rolling farmland, a great farmers market, and Alley's General Store.

Martha's Vineyard Chamber of Commerce
Vineyard Haven, 508-693-0085
mvy.com

FIVE SPOTS NOT TO MISS

Martha's Vineyard Museum

151 Lagoon Pond Rd., Vineyard Haven, 508-627-4441
mvmuseum.org

Aquinnah Cliffs and Gay Head Light

31 Aquinnah Cir., Aquinnah, 508-645-2300
mvy.com/aquinnah

The **Polly Hill Arboretum**

809 State Rd., West Tisbury, 508-693-9426
pollyhillarboretum.org

Island Alpaca Company

1 Head of the Pond Rd., Oak Bluffs, 508-693-5554
islandalpaca.com

The **Black Dog Tavern**

20 Beach St., Vineyard Haven, 508-693-9223
theblackdog.com/pages/the-black-dog-tavern

ENJOY NATURE
ON NANTUCKET

Remote and rather exclusive, Nantucket is 30 miles from the mainland and has a reputation for its wealthy residents and visitors, as well as its natural beauty. The tiny island is just 48 square miles, and 40 percent of that is conservation land. Nantucket's gorgeous beaches are famous, and even in the height of summer, you can find an uncrowded beach to park your chair.

In the early 19th century, Nantucket was the whaling capital of the world. You can see evidence of the wealth it brought to the island from the ship owners' and sea captains' elaborate mansions, many of which have been transformed into shops and inns. Nantucket Town, the center of most activity, is a National Historic District with more than 800 pre-1850 structures within its one square mile. In its captivating downtown, you'll find exclusive boutiques, upscale restaurants, and galleries. To get to the island, you can either fly (a 45-minute trip from Boston) or take a one-hour fast ferry from Hyannis on Cape Cod.

Nantucket Department of Culture & Tourism
25 Federal St., Nantucket, 508-228-0925
nantucket-ma.gov/2441/culture-tourism

NANTUCKET GEMS

Whaling Museum

13 Broad St., Nantucket, 508-228-1894
nha.org/visit/museums-and-tours/whaling-museum

Coskata-Coatue Wildlife Refuge and Great Point Light

Wauwinet Road, Nantucket, 508-228-5646
thetrustees.org/place/coskata-coatue-wildlife-refuge

Nantucket Shipwreck & Lifesaving Museum

158 Polpis Rd., Nantucket, 508-228-1885
eganmaritime.org/shipwreck-lifesaving-museum

Nantucket Atheneum

1 India St., Nantucket, 508-228-1110
nantucketatheneum.org

Monomoy National Wildlife Refuge

30 Wikis Way, Chatham, 508-945-0594
fws.gov/refuge/monomoy

Converse

SHOPPING AND FASHION

FAN OUT
AT FANEUIL HALL

Faneuil Hall Marketplace, Faneuil Hall, and Quincy Market justifiably confuse people, but they are located in the same place, so many people refer to all of it as Faneuil Hall. It's a hub of history, shops, and food. Historic Faneuil Hall, a.k.a. "The Cradle of Liberty," has hosted all sorts of political and civic events throughout the centuries, including speeches by Samuel Adams, George Washington, Susan B. Anthony, and others. It's a stop on the Freedom Trail, and you can visit the Ancient and Honorable Artillery Company Museum and Armory upstairs.

Faneuil Hall Marketplace has dozens of vendors, with independent shops, pushcarts with Boston-centric goods, and lots of buskers and street performers entertaining the crowds just outside. Quincy Market has food stalls cooking up everything from chowder to lobster rolls. There are also some sit-down restaurants and other attractions. Don't let Bostonians, who may call it a tourist trap, dissuade you from visiting. It's definitely worth it.

4 South Market, Boston, 617-523-1300
faneuilhallmarketplace.com

HIGHLIGHTS OF THE HALL

Best of Boston

Souvenirs, clothes, and gifts.

Neighborhoods

Boston and New England–themed shop.

I Love Boston Sports

Anything a Boston sports fan might want.

The Black Dog

An iconic brand from Martha's Vineyard.

Newbury Comics

Legendary local company with comics, music, magazines, and more.

HOBNOB
ON NEWBURY STREET

The one-mile, eight-block-long Newbury Street, which runs from Arlington Street to Massachusetts Avenue in the Back Bay, is one of Boston's fanciest shopping areas. It's packed with high-end stores like Anthropologie; Burberry; Chanel; Dr. Martens; Longchamp; and Shreve, Crump & Low. Boutique shops, restaurants, bars, cafés, juice bars, galleries, ice cream shops, and salons are also found on the busy street.

The outdoor bar and restaurant patio scene is well-known and is quite the place for people-watching (or being watched by people passing by). On Sundays in the summer, the whole stretch is closed to vehicles, so it becomes like a lively pedestrian-only street fair. Just one block away is Boylston Street, where you can find more shops and restaurants. One block in the other direction is the Commonwealth Avenue Mall, where you can take a break from the bustle under shady trees on the pretty boulevard packed with statues.

Newbury Street, Boston
newburystboston.com

ICONIC SPOTS ON THE STREET

Alan Bilzerian

34 Newbury St., 617-536-1001
alanbilzerian.com

Fish & Bone

217 Newbury St., 857-753-4176
thefishandbone.com

LIT Boutique

223 Newbury St., 617-421-8637
litboutique.com

Bobbles & Lace

225 Newbury St., 857-239-9202
bobblesandlace.com

Johnny Cupcakes

332 Newbury St., 617-375-0100
johnnycupcakes.com

86

TAKE 10
AT TRIDENT BOOKSELLERS & CAFE

Against all odds in this day and age, this vibrant, independent, family-owned Newbury Street shop has remained a gathering spot, or "third place," since 1984. Third places are places that aren't home or work, but somewhere else to be, learn, or just relax. Trident has a great selection of new and used books, unique and hard-to-find magazines, and funky gifts. The shop hosts a wealth of intellectual events, from book readings to author Q and As to book clubs to movie screenings. Trivia, poetry open-mic nights, speed dating events, and more are also on deck at the busy bookstore.

The excellent café, where you can read to your heart's content while sipping on a glass of wine or dining on something from the all-day breakfast menu, is another reason to visit. There's also an extensive lunch and dinner menu, as well as a full bar and excellent coffee, tea, and juices.

338 Newbury St., Boston, 617-267-8688
tridentbookscafe.com

BE CHARMED
IN CHATHAM

For a small-town scene, complete with candy stores and independent shops, you couldn't ask for a better place than Chatham, a charming community on Cape Cod that's just 16 square miles. Walk down Main Street to find boutiques, cafés, galleries, and restaurants galore. You'll be able to pick up unique locally made Cape Cod souvenirs, artwork, jewelry, and other specialties. Visit Chatham Pottery, known for its hydrangea-inspired stoneware collection, for a unique keepsake.

The Mayflower, an upscale general store, offers everything from candles to toys to local art. And just try to get out of the Chatham Candy Manor, in business for almost seven decades, without some of its excellent chocolate in hand. Bookstores, coffee shops, and cafés offer welcome respite when you need a rest. Even just window shopping in Chatham and taking in the architecture, with sea captains' houses, historic churches, and museums, is an experience itself.

Chatham Chamber of Commerce, 508-945-5199
chathaminfo.com

88

SAUNTER
AROUND SOWA

SoWa is the area of Boston's South End known as the neighborhood's art and design district, with about two dozen galleries in a two-block radius, plus restaurants, studios, showrooms, and boutiques housed in reclaimed industrial warehouses. First Fridays, held the first Friday of every month, are a fun and lively way to find new original artwork from local artists.

SoWa Open Market runs from May through October on Sundays, with more than 175 local artists, farmers, food trucks, brewers, and musicians. It always feels like a block party. And the year-round Vintage Market, also open on Sundays, is a treasure hunt, where you can shop for antiques, collectibles, clothing, art, and one-of-a-kind items you'd never find in a regular shop. There's also a fun winter festival, which runs from the end of November to late December inside the restored 1891 power station, itself a cool architectural gem.

Harrison Avenue, Boston, 857-378-4449
sowaboston.com

SHOPS TO VISIT YEAR-ROUND

Flock

274 Shawmut Ave., 617-391-0222
flockboston.com

Bos. Shop South End

623 Tremont St., 617-997-7097
blackownedbos.com

Stitch and Tickle

63 Thayer St., 617-792-0792
stitchandtickle.com

Gifted

2 Dartmouth St., 617-716-9924
giftedboston.com

Lekker Home

38 Wareham St., 617-737-7307
lekkerhome.com

CHECK OUT
CHARLES STREET

Historic Beacon Hill, with its cobblestone streets, historic brownstones, and the gold-domed Massachusetts State House, is a must-see neighborhood for its storied past, but it's also a great place to go shopping. The main shopping drag is Charles Street, located just across from Boston Common, running from Beacon Street up to Cambridge Street. It is packed with adorable shops, specializing in everything from antiques to clothing to souvenirs. December Thieves, the Flat of the Hill, and Rugg Road Paper Company are among some of the more established shops, offering all sorts of unique items. There are plenty of places to eat and drink along the street, too. Pop into the Liberty Hotel, which was once a prison but is now a luxurious property with nods to its former life in its expansive lobby, and restaurant Alibi and bar Clink.

Beacon Hill, Boston

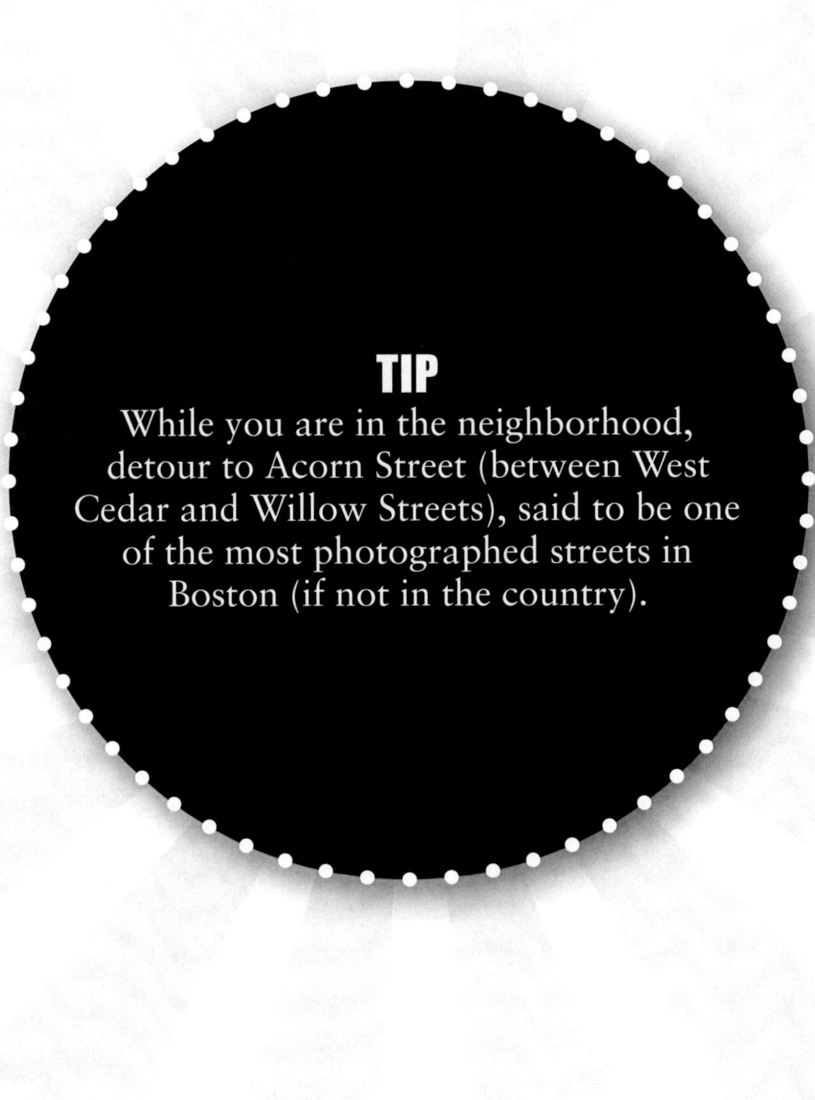

TIP

While you are in the neighborhood, detour to Acorn Street (between West Cedar and Willow Streets), said to be one of the most photographed streets in Boston (if not in the country).

BROWSE
AT BEACON HILL BOOKS

Like Trident Booksellers, Beacon Hill Books & Cafe is so much more than a bookstore. It's a gathering spot, a hangout, and a place to savor a meal or afternoon tea. The four-story building in historic Beacon Hill offers all the magic you could want in a bookstore, with little nooks to sit in and a working fireplace on every floor. It feels more like a friend's townhouse who perhaps has an intense passion for books (like, a lot of books). The bottom floor is the café and wine bar, with indoor and outdoor seating, with the other three floors dedicated to books. Even if you don't need a kids book, don't skip the charming children's section on the top floor. There's a reasonably priced prix fixe menu for dinner and afternoon tea, while breakfast and lunch are à la carte. Author readings, signings, and talks are offered on a regular basis.

71 Charles St., Boston, 617-945-4713
bhbooks.com

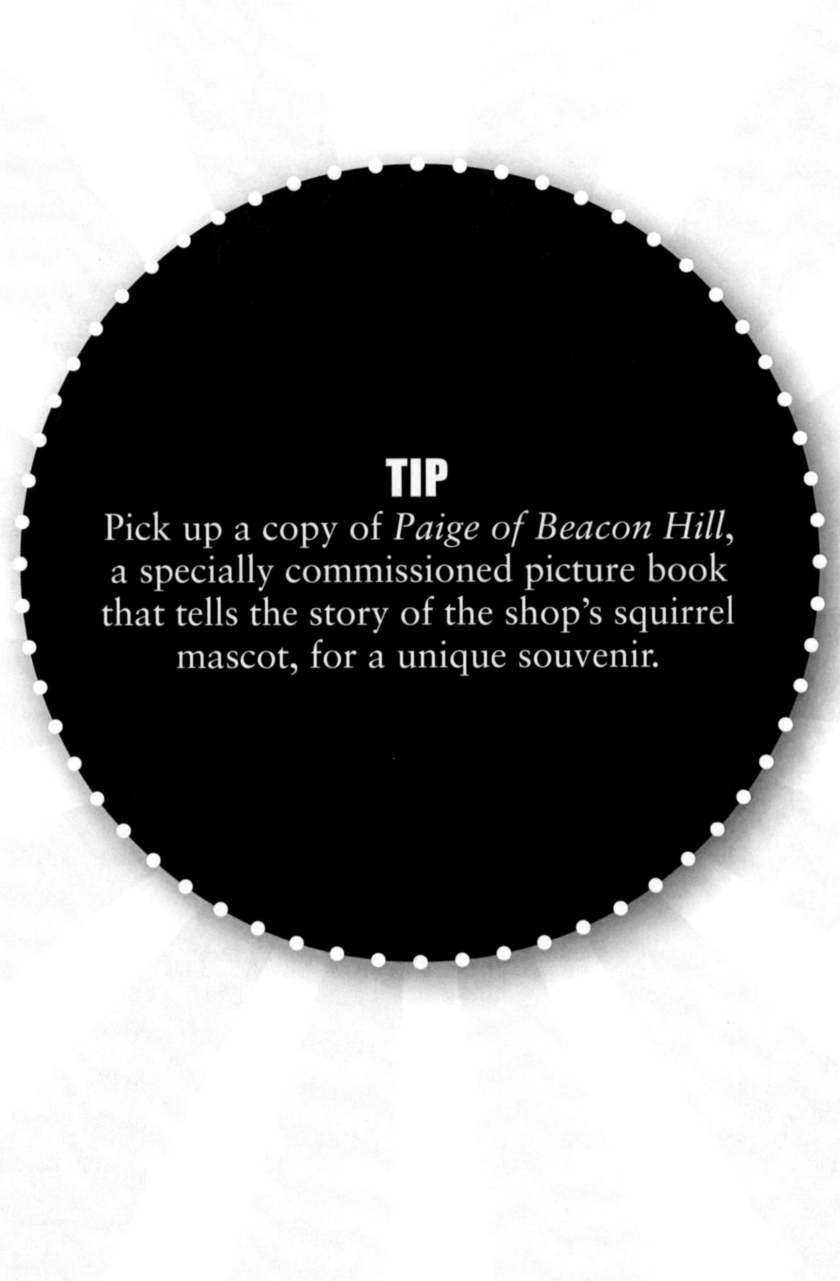

TIP

Pick up a copy of *Paige of Beacon Hill*, a specially commissioned picture book that tells the story of the shop's squirrel mascot, for a unique souvenir.

CUSTOMIZE YOUR KICKS
AT CONVERSE

While the Converse brand is well-known, not everyone knows it was launched in 1908 in Malden, Massachusetts. Practically synonymous with basketball players, musicians, and celebrities, the brand started off making rubber galoshes! In 1915, a focus on athletic shoes moved the company in a new direction, and when Charles H. "Chuck" Taylor joined Converse in 1921, he was a huge fan and promoter of the All-Star basketball sneaker, and well, the rest is history.

Today, you can visit the Converse Flagship Store on Lovejoy Wharf, within steps of TD North Garden, and design your own sneakers. While you can also customize them online, it is so much more fun to do it in person, with the super-friendly designers on hand to walk you through styles, colors, patches, wording, materials, and other ways to make your sneakers uniquely you. And if you just want a regular pair of sneakers, there are a lot to choose from off the shelf.

1 Lovejoy Wharf, Boston, 617-248-9530
converse.com

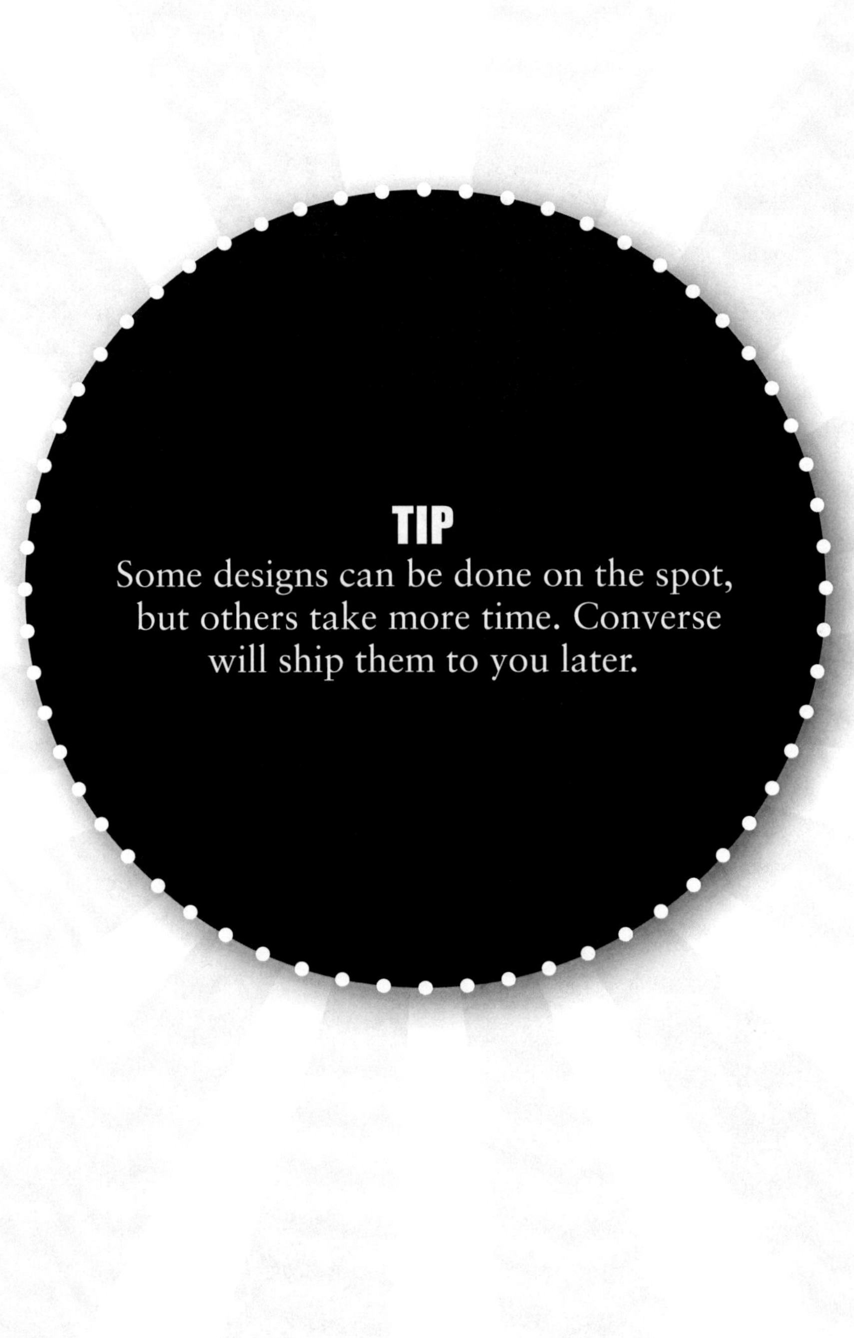
TIP
Some designs can be done on the spot, but others take more time. Converse will ship them to you later.

BOOK IT
TO BROOKLINE BOOKSMITH

Brookline Booksmith is yet one more excellent and much-loved bookstore in the Boston area. Located in the heart of Coolidge Corner, the 12,500-square-foot shop, which opened in 1961, has been the go-to spot for books, community, and cultural events for decades. There is a huge selection of books, from the newest bestsellers to classic paperbacks to comic books. Downstairs, you'll find the Used Book Cellar, where customers can buy and sell gently used books, and you never know what gem you'll find in the bargain book section.

The store hosts more than 300 author talks annually, community conversations, and book clubs, with big-name authors making appearances. In addition to books, there's a large and well-curated selection of gift items, from calendars to foodstuffs to notebooks and diaries to jewelry. No matter the occasion, you can always find a present here. And if you need a book recommendation, just ask. The staff always has a well-informed opinion.

279 Harvard St., Brookline, 617-566-6660
brooklinebooksmith.com

SEARCH FOR TREASURES
AT THE CAMBRIDGE ANTIQUE MARKET

A fixture since 1991, this “market” offers five floors of treasure-hunting heaven for anyone who lives for the thrill of finding something special. There are more than 150 dealers, offering almost everything under the sun, including jewelry, books, furniture, artwork, fine silver, glassware, china, toys, vintage clothing, collectibles, lighting—the list goes on. If you are looking for a specific cast-iron pot in a particular shape, this is the place. Need to replace a Pyrex casserole dish or a piece of china from a set? You have a good chance of finding it here. Looking for unique pieces of vintage jewelry or a series of comic books for your collection? Start your search here. It’s a lot of fun to browse through each floor at your leisure, taking in all of the items once loved by someone else and now ready for a new home. You never know what you might find!

201 Monsignor O’Brien Hwy., Cambridge, 617-868-9655
cambridgeantiquemarket.com

94

BARGAIN FOR DAYS
AT BRIMFIELD

Three times a year, in May, July, and September, for six days in a row, thousands of people flock to Brimfield for the Brimfield Flea Markets to hunt for treasures, shop for antiques, and see what might catch their eye from the hundreds and hundreds of dealers. Spread across 19 fields and other venues, the event is hard to envision unless you've been in person. Every kind of item you can think of is for sale, from comic books to clothes to vintage toys to kitchen sinks (seriously!). Enormous pieces of furniture, custom artwork, heirloom jewelry, rare books, and scores of other delightful items fill the tables and tents.

In addition to all the merchandise dealers, there are food trucks, beverage carts, and plenty of places up and down Route 20 to eat and drink or take a break. The event is such a big deal that in 2024, its 65th anniversary, it was added to the National Register of Historic Places.

35 Palmer Rd., Brimfield
brimfieldantiquefleamarket.com

95

CRAFT A CANDLE
AT YANKEE CANDLE VILLAGE

If you are a candle lover, especially of unique, scented candles, you need to head to the Yankee Candle Village in Deerfield, a vast wonderland of candles that is so much more than a store. You can shop for thousands of candles in the Candle Emporium, plus all sorts of other goods, and you can also make your own candle at the Custom Candle Bar, where you create your own custom scent. Or head to the Wax Works, where you can make a wax mold of your hand or dip objects in wax. Yankee Candy has a seven-foot-tall gumball machine, homemade fudge, and 125 different types of candy to tempt you. There's a year-round Bavarian Christmas Village, featuring a 25-foot-tall Christmas tree, a six-foot-tall nutcracker, and "snow" that falls every few minutes. In addition, there's a Build-A-Bear Workshop, a café, and special events held throughout the year.

25 Greenfield Rd., South Deerfield, 877-636-7707
yankeecandle.com/south-deerfield-village.html

RAMBLE ALONG
ROCKY NECK

On the North Shore in Gloucester, Rocky Neck calls a siren song to artists. Located on a peninsula within Gloucester's working harbor, it's well known for its scenic beauty, unique light, and rich cultural history. Plein air artists, such as Winslow Homer and Edward Hopper, lived and worked on Rocky Neck in the 19th and early 20th centuries, and artists continue to be drawn to the area.

Today, there are almost two dozen galleries on the harbor, featuring the works of painters, potters, textile designers, photographers, jewelry makers, and more. It's a wonderful place to find distinctive items. There are also plenty of spots to eat, drink, and get ice cream. Pick up a map at the Cultural Center at Rocky Neck. While you're in the area, make time to head to Bearskin Neck in Rockport, another quaint village just fifteen minutes away. Look for Motif No. 1, a famous little red fishing shack on the harbor, which has been painted perhaps more than any other building in the world.

6 Wonson St., Gloucester, 978-515-7004
rockyneckculturaldistrict.org

RELAX
AT THE BOOKSTORE & GET LIT WINE BAR

Not every bookstore can say it's been the subject of a charming documentary, but the Bookstore in Lenox is not just any independent bookstore. It's been a fixture in the community for decades, and the film *Hello, Bookstore* tells the story of owner Matt Tannenbaum, who has been the heart and soul of the shop for more than 40 years, and the ups and downs of the shop.

The beloved store holds author talks regularly and exhibits artwork in its Shade Gallery. In addition, the Get Lit Wine Bar, a small area with half a dozen stools, is open whenever the bookstore is. Relaxing with a book and a glass of wine is a lovely way to spend a pleasant hour or two. And if you need a book recommendation or just want to chat, you're definitely in the right place.

11 Housatonic St., Lenox, 413-637-3390
bookstoreinlenox.com

STOCK UP
AT THE BREWSTER STORE

Since 1866, the Brewster Store, located in an 1852 church turned charming general store, has been a community hub for the neighborhood. You can find everything from candies and greeting cards to snacks to snow globes and everything in between. The well-worn wooden floors, counters, shelves, and drawers speak to its long history. This is one of those stores where it's impossible to leave without buying something, and it's probably something you didn't come in to buy!

Out front, benches are popular with locals and visitors, where you can sit a spell and enjoy a cup of coffee or some homemade ice cream from the adjacent Brewster Scoop. Whether you need a sweatshirt for chilly nights, a jigsaw puzzle for rainy days, a keepsake ornament to take home, a book to read on the beach, toys for the kids, or just a snack, this is the spot to find it.

1935 Main St., Brewster, 508-896-3744
brewsterstore.com

TAKE YOUR TIME
AT TITCOMB'S

This charming family-owned bookstore in East Sandwich on Cape Cod is chockablock with new and old books, toys, gifts, and cards. The three-story bookstore, which was built by two of the Titcomb sons, is a cherished part of the community, with a busy schedule of author talks and readings. The origin story of the bookstore is quite a story itself. In the 1960s, the Titcomb children discovered a collection of rare papers and books in their barn in Connecticut. This led to the family starting a mail-order catalog business, and over the years, it grew and grew.

When the family moved to the Cape in 1969, they opened a brick-and-mortar shop, and it's as popular as ever. Don't miss a photo op with the statue of the colonial man out front, also made by one of the Titcomb sons. It's a tradition for visiting authors, such as Geraldine Brooks, Jodi Picoult, and others, to pose by it when they come for book signings.

432 MA-6A, East Sandwich, 508-888-2331
titcombsbookshop.com

STROLL
ON COMMERCIAL STREET

The main avenue in Provincetown is Commercial Street, which is packed with shops, galleries, studios, restaurants, cafés, bakeries, bars, and boutiques. The compact, historically LGBTQ+-friendly town must be explored by foot, and you can get there by fast ferry if you are coming from Boston. The lively center of town is ideal for people-watching, especially in the bustling summer season.

The East End boasts a number of nationally renowned galleries, while the West End has a number of small inns and B and Bs. You can find art in all mediums, from fine art paintings to marine life to wooden sculptures to abstract works, and everything in between. For a selection of works by more than 30 artists, stop in at the Cortile Gallery. There are plenty of gift shops and other specialty stores to pop into, as well.

Commercial Street, Provincetown
ptowntourism.com

MORE PROVINCETOWN HIGHLIGHTS

Arcadia

131 Commercial St., 774-538-6046
arcadiaptown.com

Provincetown Bookshop

229 Commercial St., 508-487-0964
provincetownbookshop.com

Egeli Gallery

382 Commercial St., 508-487-0044
egeligallery.com

Gallery 444

444 Commercial St., 617-710-2026
gallery444ptown.com

John Derian

Law St. (back of 396 Commercial St.), 508-487-1362
johnderian.com

1964
NEW YORK
SCHIFF'S
SCHIFF'S
SCHIFF'S
ALLSPICE
THE HOOD BASIC COOK BOOK
HESELTINE and DOW
15¢

Brimfield

ACTIVITIES BY SEASON

WINTER

SPRING

SUMMER

FALL

SUGGESTED ITINERARIES

ART LOVERS

FOODIES

HISTORY BUFFS

SUMMER FUN

SEAFOOD FANS

INDEX

James Hook & Co.